TWO CLASSICAL C

ARISTOPHANES

The Birds

PLAUTUS

The Brothers Menaechmus

TRANSLATED AND EDITED BY

Peter D. Arnott

TUFTS UNIVERSITY

Harlan Davidson, Inc.
Arlington Heights, Illinois 60004

LIBRARY OF CONGRESS CATALOGING-IN-PUBLICATION DATA

Two classical comedies.

  (Crofts classics)
  Bibliography: p.
  Contents: The birds / Aristophanes — The Brothers
Menaechmus / Plautus.
  1. Classical drama (Comedy)—Translations into
English. 2. English drama (Comedy)—Translations from
classical languages. I. Arnott, Peter D.
II. Aristophanes. Birds. English. 1986.
III. Plautus, Titus Maccius. Menaechmi. English.
1986.
PA3629.T86   1986   882'.01'08   86-2171
ISBN 0-88295-004-5 (pbk.)

Manufactured in the United States of America
95 94 93 92 91 EB 18 19 20 21

INTRODUCTION

ARISTOPHANES AND GREEK COMEDY

THE ORIGINS of Greek comedy are obscure. It began perhaps in rustic celebrations, where choruses of villagers,
sometimes dressed as animals, sang and danced, poking
fun at local institutions and celebrities. This spirit of ir-
reverence persists throughout Greek comedy at its best,
and the chorus remained the most important feature.
Other recurring elements in the literary drama, such as
the *agon*, a debate or contest, and the *parabasis*, where
the chorus addresses the audience on current affairs quite
irrelevant to the plot, may derive from such improvised
celebrations. Epicharmus of Sicily (540-450 B.C.) wrote
comedies of everyday life which burlesqued both men
and gods, and a similar form of drama was known at
Megara. Probably all these influences helped to shape
Greek comedy as we know it.

We possess only eleven complete comedies, all by
Aristophanes. Other writers, some more successful than
Aristophanes in their lifetime, survive only in tantalizing
fragments. He was born about 450 B.C., when comedy
had become a recognized part of the great Athenian dramatic festivals, and lived through the war with Sparta
which ended with the subjugation of Athens in 404 and
the loss of her proud position as the leader of Greece.
The progress of the war with its increasing hardship gave
him several of his themes, and the deteriorating political
situation left its mark upon his later work. He cannot be
tied to any particular party. His frequent attacks on in-
novations in politics, philosophy, and the theater have
been cited as evidence for his conservatism, but a comic
poet must have something to be funny about, and the
leading personalities of the day were obvious targets. He
was always willing to attack famous figures of the older

generation, like Aeschylus or Pericles, when the need arose.

The theater for which he wrote was the same as for tragedy—a circular *orchestra*, or dancing-floor, for the chorus, backed by a few steps rising to a low platform which gave extra height for the actors. Behind this was the scene-building, a permanent architectural façade with doors which could represent houses, palaces, caves, or anything demanded by the play. There was no painted scenery. The words were enough to establish the setting, and action flowed swiftly from scene to scene without interruption. Actors were masked, and so could change roles quickly. They wore short, easy-fitting tunics which were often grotesquely padded. There was much use of the stock stage machinery—cranes which hoisted characters into the air to represent flight, and movable platforms pushed out from the scene-building to display tableaux.

Aristophanes' first two plays—*The Banqueters* (427 B.C.) and *The Babylonians*—no longer survive. *The Acharnians* (425) which won first prize at the festival makes fun of the war. An elderly Athenian, tired of restrictions, negotiates a private peace with Sparta and opens his own market. Trade thrives, and the play ends on a hilarious contrast; at one side of the stage the old man enjoys a banquet while at the other a general prepares for the miseries of war. Next year saw *The Knights* with a more personal target, the demagogue Cleon, who represented the new element in Athenian politics. A man of the people, he lacked the dignity and restraint which marked Athenian statesmanship of earlier years. It is said that the mask-maker, frightened of reprisals, refused to make his likeness. *The Clouds*, a burlesque of Socrates and the new philosophy, followed in 423. It was unsuccessful, and we possess only a rewritten version that may never have been performed. Perhaps the first version was above the heads of the audience. In 424 came *The Wasps*, satirizing the Athenian love of litigation, and in 421 *The Peace*, in which another old Athenian, a shrewd, humorous old man of the type Aristophanes loved to draw, mounts to heaven on a beetle to drag Peace from the well into which War has thrown her. In fact a peace

was ratified with Sparta soon after this production, but
did not last for long.

A gap of seven years follows before our next surviving
play, *The Birds,* in 414. This represents in many ways
the high-water mark of Aristophanes' achievement. Schol-
ars have tried to find in it an elaborate allegory of the
current political situation, but at most it reflects the general feeling of the times. A great expedition to Sicily was
in preparation and it seemed that Athens' fortunes might
improve at last. The play is in a mood of high fantasy,
and contains some of Aristophanes' most bizarre invention and most beautiful poetry. It contains topical references, it is true, but it would be wrong to see it as anything other than a romantic extravaganza. The topicalities
are noticeably fewer than in other plays, a fact which
makes *The Birds* easier to appreciate today. Surprisingly,
it won only second prize.

These plays sum up all that is best in "Old Comedy"
as it is known, and this is a convenient point at which to
summarize Aristophanes' style, as afterwards the character of his work changes. As an art-form Old Comedy
remains unique. Aristophanes resembles the Marx Brothers
more than Molière. His plays are amazingly versatile.
They jump from broad farce to polished wit, from obscene
fooling to beautiful lyrics, in the space of a few lines,
and one is never conscious of the abruptness of the transi-
tion. Plots are tenuous and inconsequent, a series of comic
episodes linked by a central character or theme. Into
these fantasies are inserted references to Athenian life
and affairs, to politics and the war; members of the audience are mentioned by name and parodied on the stage.
Even the gods are not immune; the Athenians saw no
harm in allowing their deities to be publicly mocked.
Perhaps the closest modern parallel is to be found in the
Gilbert and Sullivan operas. Old Comedy was at the same
time pure entertainment and penetrating satire, a valu-
able medium of social comment, written in verse highly
spiced with slang and echoing the language of the street
and market-place.

Lysistrata (411) marks a change in method. It was no
longer safe to be outspoken. Although the city was in a

ferment, with political cliques plotting and counterplotting and even resorting to open violence, there is no hint of this in the play. True, it is another attack on the folly of war—the women of the opposing states refuse to associate with their husbands until they stop fighting—but it lacks the personal note that marked the earlier plays.

Thesmophoriazusae (*Mothers' Day*), performed in the following spring, returns to personalities, but these are only literary. The butt is Euripides, the tragic poet, in danger of his life from the women of Athens because of his harsh portrayal of them in his plays. He appears again in *The Frogs* (405). Dionysus, God of Tragedy, visits the Underworld and judges a contest between Euripides and his predecessor Aeschylus, an excuse for elaborate satire on the style of both authors.

Before the next play, *Ecclesiazousae* (*Women in Parliament*), Athens had fallen and the poet's freedom was finally curbed. This and his last play, *Wealth*, are amusing but no longer stimulating; the sting has gone out of them.

It is unfortunate that one of Aristophanes' chief virtues as a comic poet, his topicality, should prevent us from fully enjoying his work today. The more topical a play at first performance, the more quickly it loses its flavor. Many of his jokes are no longer funny to us because we do not know the people about whom they were written. Yet a great deal remains, and it is a tribute to his lasting powers as an entertainer that we can still laugh at the humor that first amused the citizens of Athens 2500 years ago.

PLAUTUS AND ROMAN COMEDY

Roman comedy was derived directly from Greek, but not from Aristophanes. After the defeat of Athens, less secure and therefore less tolerant governments could no longer permit the freedom that marked the earlier comic stage. Satire's edge was blunted. Playwrights, no longer able to attack the state and its institutions, turned their wit into safer channels. The result was an innocuous comedy of manners, with Menander as its chief exponent.

It exploited the dramatic possibilities of romantic love. Plots turned on thwarted marriages, parted lovers, reconciliations and happy endings. Mistaken identity was a frequent motivation. In Menander's *The Rape of the Locks* a soldier suspects his mistress of infidelity and punishes her by cutting off her hair. It afterwards turns out that the supposed lover was her brother. *The Arbitration* deals with the parentage of an abandoned baby who is claimed by two contending parties.

This simple formula was capable of infinite variation. Characters fall into sharply defined types, each obvious from his appropriate costume and mask—angry old man, placid old man, young lover, courtesan, cunning slave, and so forth. The chorus declined sharply in importance. Its songs deprived of their topicality, there was little reason for it to exist. It was no longer an integral part of the play but a mere divertissement, whose sole function was to enliven the action with an occasional irrelevant song and dance. All that remained was the note "Chorus" inserted in the manuscript to indicate that at this point the chorus was to enter and sing, it mattered not what.

These plays, the "New Comedy," were widely acted both in Greece itself and the flourishing Greek colonies of southern Italy. In addition to performances in the permanent theaters, traveling companies took them on tour, performing on fit-up stages wherever there was an audience. When the Romans pushed southward they found this wealth of dramatic material awaiting them, and lost no time in adapting it to their purpose. "Conquered Greece," says Horace, "subdued its savage captor." The native genius of the Romans, as yet crude and unpolished but suggesting great possibilities, succumbed before these finished products of a mature culture. Roman playwrights brought these works to their own stage, sometimes spiced with topical allusions but retaining their Greek form and character. Two Greek plays could be combined into one, a process known as *contaminatio.*

Theater buildings had shared in the change. With the chorus no longer important, there was no need for an *orchestra.* Some were reduced to a semicircle, others used for additional seating. That of the Theater of Dionysus at Athens eventually suffered the ultimate degradation, being made watertight to accommodate mimic naval battles. As the actors became more prominent the stage was made higher, but an architectural background was still all that was required; the action of New Comedy commonly passed in front of houses or in a street. The first Roman theaters, for which Plautus wrote, copied the form of the Greek but were made of wood. Play-acting was still regarded with suspicion, and it was thought that a permanent theater would encourage time-wasting and frivolity. Rome had no permanent stone theater until 55 B.C.

Titus Maccius Plautus typified this new spirit in the drama. Born about 254 B.C. at Sarsina in Umbria, and thus, like so many of Rome's greatest men, a provincial, he was more wholly a man of the theater than his Greek predecessors in that he wrote for a living. Little is known about his life. Tradition has it that he worked as a stage carpenter, making a little money which he afterwards lost in a rash investment. Poverty forced him to work in a flour mill, where he found time to write plays. He was successful both during his life and for long after his death in 184. An immense number of plays were attributed to him, theatrical managers hoping to borrow glory from his name, but the only genuine ones are probably the twenty we now possess.

He was in every sense a popular dramatist who knew what the public wanted and gave it to them, in marked contrast to his successor Terence, whose pure style and more subtle wit were above the heads of his audience. Plautus' plays are full of broad humor and farcical situations. There is rarely any depth of characterization, though Plautus could at times write with feeling, as in *Captivi* (*Prisoners of War*), where an old father discovers that his son is working for him as a slave. He has few literary graces, though he can conjure up a striking phrase. For this reason Plautus suffers perhaps more than any other author from being read rather than performed. His genius lies in his ability to handle a plot. His plays are wonders of craftsmanship. Highly complicated, they are never obscure, and the spectator is kept amused and intrigued to the end.

Most of the plays are variations on the familiar theme

of credulous old men, rascally sons and cunning slaves, but four in particular, besides *Captivi,* stand out. *Rudens,* (*The Rope*), tells how a well-born lady of Athens, kidnapped at birth, is saved from a procurer's hands by her lover. The high moral tone of this comedy and the refreshing simplicity of its rural setting set it apart from the rest. *Aulularia* (*Buried Treasure*), from which Molière took his *L'Avare,* has a brilliant comic portrait of a man crazed by sudden wealth. *Miles Gloriosus* (*Captain Cocksure*) contains one of the best examples of a popular New Comic type, the soldier who prefers boasting to fighting.

Menaechmi (*The Brothers Menaechmus*) shows Plautus at his best. We do not know when it was written—attempts to date it rest on very slender evidence—but it has all the ingredients of success, an ingenious plot, boldly contrasted characters, and, above all, a sheer comic exuberance that defies criticism. Plautus' sources are also unknown. There were at least six different Greek plays entitled *Twins.* Much of the Greek characterization is preserved. Messenio, for example, harangues his master with a Greek freedom, and the Parasite, a professional sponger who gives flattery in return for meals, was at this time still a purely Greek type. The client-patron relationship, on the other hand, about which Menaechmus complains so bitterly, was Roman. Freed slaves, aliens, and others attached themselves as retainers to some rich man. It was a social distinction to have many clients.

Plautus' success in handling his material may best be seen by comparison with Shakespeare's *Comedy of Errors,* partially based on this play. Shakespeare complicates the plot still further by adding a second set of twins, but this does not entirely excuse the confusion in which the spectator finds himself. In Plautus one is never in doubt as to which twin is on the stage; even if they did not announce themselves, the acquisitiveness of Menaechmus of Syracuse is sufficiently contrasted with the stupidity of his Epidamnian brother. Besides Shakespeare's there have been several other imitations, and in modern performances the *Menaechmi* deservedly remains the most popular of Plautus' plays.

The Birds

and

The Brothers Menaechmus

DRAMATIS PERSONAE

❊

EUELPIDES ("Hopeful")
PISTHETAIRUS ("Blarney") } elderly Athenians
A Bird, servant to TEREUS.
TEREUS, once a King, changed by the gods into a Hoopoe.
CHORUS OF BIRDS
A Poet
A Soothsayer
METON
A Commissioner
A Statute-seller
IRIS, Goddess of Rainbows, heavenly messenger.
A Son who beats his father.
CINESIAS, a minstrel.
An Informer
PROMETHEUS
POSEIDON, God of Oceans.
HERACLES, a demi-god.
TRIBALLIAN, a barbarian god.
      Sentries, Messengers, Slaves, and Stagehands.

SCENE: A high and deserted spot, the Kingdom of the Birds.

Aristophanes

THE BIRDS

❧

[*Enter* Pisthetairus *and* Euelpides, *staggering under
the load of luggage—including a full range of kitchen
equipment—that they carry on their backs. Each carries
a bird, to help him scent out the way*]

EUELP. [*To his bird*] Straight on, you tell me, where
the tree-trunk is?

PISTH. Confound this bird, he's croaking in reverse.

EUELP. Why all this roaming up and down, you beast?
We're on a shuttle service to destruction!

PISTH. What misery to have this crow for guide!
I've covered a hundred miles or more today.

EUELP. What wretched luck to have this daw for
guide—
I've worn my toe-nails to the bone with walking!

PISTH. Well, I can't tell you where on earth we are
now.

EUELP. Could you get back to mother Athens now?   10

PISTH. By Zeus, not even Execestides could do so!

EUELP. Damnation!

PISTH. That's where you'll end up, old boy.

EUELP. That oaf Philocrates, the market man
Who sells the birds, has made fools out of us!
He told us they'd divine where Tereus lived,

[11] **By Zeus** Pisthetairus commonly swears by the Father of the
Gods, but Heracles, Apollo, Poseidon, and others are used
frequently for oaths in this play **Execestides** an unqualified
person who had somehow acquired Athenian citizenship; see
v. 1423 [15] **Tereus** legendary king of Thrace ravished Procne
and married her sister Philomela; in revenge they killed his
son Itys and served him up for his father's dinner. Tereus pur-
sued them and all three were changed into birds, hoopoe,
nightingale, and swallow respectively.

1

The hoopoe, who turned bird in borrowed feathers,
And sold this chick off Tharraleides' block,
This crow, for ten cents, and this jackdaw for a quarter,
And all they bother their heads about is biting!

20 [*To his bird*] Now what are you gaping at? Here goes!
Over the rocks again! There's no road here,
Not anywhere.

    PISTH.   By Zeus, not even a track.
    EUELP. Doesn't your crow say anything about the road?
    PISTH. By Zeus, it's croaking a different tune just now.
    EUELP. What does it say about the road?
    PISTH.   Why, just one thing—
He'll take a bite and have my fingers off!

    EUELP. Isn't it tragic we should come prepared
And wanting nothing but to get the bird,
Then be unable to find out the way?

30 For we, good audience, are sick with a disease
Quite opposite to that which Sacas had—
A displaced person, whom no state would take
Until at last he elbowed into ours.
But we're of honest birth and well-connected,
As good as the next man; we haven't been shooed off,
But flew away from Athens—on our feet.
Not that we hate the city we've abandoned,
Not that it isn't great, and heaven-blessed,
And quite impartial in collecting fines!

40 The cicalas perch on the branches singing
A month or two; but the men of Athens
Spend lungpower in the lawcourts all their lives.
That's why we packed our holy jug and basket
And myrtle wreaths, and started on our march.
We're looking round for some untroubled place
Where we can settle down and rusticate.
Our expedition is in search of Tereus
The hoopoe, wanting information from him
If he's had a birds-eye-view of some such place.

    PISTH. I say!
    EUELP.   What do you want?

---

[17] **Tharraleides** unknown   [31] **Sacas** nickname of Acestor the tragic poet, who had Scythian blood   [40] **cicalas** (or **cicadas**) a chirping insect common in Greece   [43] **holy . . . wreaths** for offering sacrifice when founding a new colony

PISTH.   This crow of mine's 50
Been croaking "Up!" for ages.
EUELP.   And this jackdaw here
Is gaping in the air, to show me something.
There must be birds here, that's a certainty.
We'll know directly if we make a noise.

PISTH. I tell you—bang your foot against a rock.

EUELP. You use your head, and there'll be twice the
noise.

PISTH. Take a stone and knock.

EUELP.   All right, if you think so. Porter! Porter!

PISTH. What are you saying? Calling the hoopoe
"porter"?
You ought to shout "Whoopo! whoopo!" not "porter"!

EUELP. Whoopo! whoopo! Must I knock again?
Whoopo!   60

[*Enter a* BIRD, *so suddenly that the two men fall down
in fright. He is fantastically dressed—as are all the* BIRDS
—with a big gaping beak.]

BIRD. Who's that? Who's shouting for my master?

EUELP. Apollo be my saviour, what a gape!

BIRD. Oh dear, oh dear, the birdcatchers have come!

EUELP. This creature's bark's no better than his bite.

BIRD. You'll die!

EUELP.   But we're not men.

BIRD.   What are you, then?

EUELP. I'm the Scared-to-death, a Libyan bird.

BIRD. What sort of a bird are you? Well, lost your
tongue?

PISTH. The Nightjar, of the pheasant family.

EUELP. What manner of thing are you, in heaven's
name?

BIRD. A slave bird.

EUELP.   Did you lose a cockfight?

BIRD.   No! 70
But when my master turned into a hoopoe
He begged me to become a bird as well
To have someone to follow and attend him.

---

[70] **Lose a cock-fight** prisoners of war were sold as slaves: Euelpides assumes that this bird has lost a battle

EUELP. Do birds need servants, just like men?
BIRD.   He does,
Because he's been a man himself, I think.
Sometimes he craves Phalerian sardines.
I take a bowl, and run for the sardines.
He fancies porridge, needs his dish and spoon—
I run to get the spoon.
    EUELP.   A secretary bird!
80 Now secretary, I'll dictate! Go call
Your master to us.
    BIRD.   By Zeus, he's fast asleep
After his gnat and myrtleberry dinner.
    EUELP. I don't care—wake him up!
    BIRD.   He won't be pleased,
I'm sure, but since it's you—I'll do it. [Exit]
    PISTH. I hope you rot! You frightened me to death!
    EUELP. Oh, curse it, here's bad luck. I was so scared
My daw escaped.
    PISTH.   You mouse! You lost your daw
Because you were so frightened?
    EUELP.   Where's your crow?
Didn't you let it loose when you fell down?
    PISTH. Not I, by Zeus.
    EUELP.   Where is it, then?
90 PISTH.   Flown off.

[The HOOPOE is heard, declaiming in the pompous tones
of a tragedian]

    HOOP. Come, part the grove that I may issue forth.

[He enters]

    EUELP. Great Heracles, what's here? What creature's
        this?
Those feathers! What's this triple crest he's wearing?
    HOOP. Who seek me?
    EUELP.   It seems the twelve Olympians
Have had it in for you.

---

[76] **Phalerian sardines** possibly anchovies, a great delicacy
[84] **twelve Olympians** the supreme council of the gods

HOOP.   Do you mock me
Because you see me feathered? Strangers, I
Was once a man.
    EUELP.   It's not you we're laughing at.
    HOOP. What then?
    EUELP.   We found your beak amusing.
    HOOP. Yet Sophocles delights to mock me so,   100
As Tereus in his tragedies.
    EUELP. You're Tereus? Are you bird or dodo?
    HOOP. I am a bird.
    EUELP.   Where are your feathers then?
    HOOP. All moulted.
    EUELP.   Sickening for some disease?
    HOOP. No, all we birds lose feathers in the winter.
And then grow others to make up the loss.
But tell me who you are.
    EUELP.   We? We're men!
    HOOP. What country?
    EUELP.   Where the finest fleet comes from.
    HOOP. Not magistrates?
    EUELP.   No, quite the other sort—
We're anti-magistrates.
    HOOP.   Does that seed grow there too?
    EUELP. Search in the country and you'll find a little.   110
    HOOP. What errand brought you all the way up here?
    EUELP. We want to talk to you.
    HOOP.   And what about?
    EUELP. You were once a man yourself, as we are now,
And ran up little bills, as we do now,
And loved to get off paying, as we do now.
And then you changed your nature for a bird's
And flew the orbit of both land and sea.
You know all men know, and what birds know too,
And so we've come to ask you for assistance,
If you can tell us some well-padded spot,   120
Some feather-bed place, snug to settle down.

---

[100] **Sophocles** (495-406 B.C.) used the legend for his tragedy *Tereus* [101] **Dodo** in the Greek "peacock," then a great curiosity. The word has been changed to keep the joke. [108] **Magistrates** the litigiousness of the Athenians was notorious

Hoop. Do you seek a greater than the Cranaan town?
Euelp. Not greater, no, but one that suits us better.
Hoop. I see, you want an aristocracy.
Euelp.   Not I!
I can't abide the sight of Scellias' son.
   Hoop. What sort of place would be your favorite?
   Euelp. A place where this would be my greatest
     trouble—
One of my friends comes early to my door
And says something like this: "By Olympian Zeus,
130 Take your baths good and early today,
You and your children—there's a wedding breakfast
     going!
Let nothing put you off. But if you do,
Don't dare come near me when my money's gone!"
   Hoop. By Zeus, you are in love with troubles!
There's a flourishing city of the sort you mention
On the Red Sea coast.
   Euelp.   No, that would never do.
We'd never like the coast, where every dawn
Might bring a boat with extradition papers.
   Hoop. Why not go to Elis to live
In Lepreum?
140   Euelp.   Heavens, no! I've never seen it
But I've seen Melanthius. Leprous! Not for me!
   Hoop. Well, what of the Opuntians in Locris?
A charming neighborhood!
   Euelp.   No place for me.
I wouldn't be Opuntius for a fortune.
What sort of life is this among the birds?
You know first hand.
   Hoop.   It's easy on the pocket
To start with—we've no use for money here.
   Euelp. No money! Then no lies—or not so many.
   Hoop. A vegetarian diet—myrtle berries,
150 White sesame, and thyme, and poppy seed.

---

[122] **Cranaan town** the oldest name of Athens [125] **Scellias' son**
the choice of a town provides an excuse for puns on the names
of unpopular Athenians. They will not have an aristocracy because of Aristocrates, son of Scellias, go to Lepreum because of Melanthius the leper or to the Opuntians because of
Opuntius the informer

EUELP. Your life is one long wedding breakfast then.

PISTH. I say! I say!
This land of birds has given me ideas.
Do as I tell you and you'll all be kings.

HOOP. What do you mean?

PISTH.   What do I mean? Well, first
Stop flying everywhere with mouths wide open.
It brings you into disrepute. Where we come from,
On earth, someone will ask the flighty folk
"Now who's this bird?" and Teleas will reply
"The man's a bird, a flutterer, never still,   160
Inconstant, not the same two minutes running."

HOOP. By Dionysus, that rebuke's deserved.
What should we do then?

PISTH.   Found yourselves one city.

HOOP. Where should we found a city for the birds?

PISTH. Are you in earnest? What an asinine remark.
Look down.

HOOP.   I'm looking.

PISTH.   Now look up above.

HOOP. I am.

PISTH.   Now twist your neck around.

HOOP.   By Zeus
Much good it will do me if I choke myself.

PISTH. What did you see?

HOOP.   The heavens and the clouds.

PISTH. And isn't what you see the bird's economy?   170

HOOP. Economy?

PISTH.   Their sphere, as one might say.
We call it your economy because
It stretches out so far.
Blockade it, build a city in the sky
And make of this economy autonomy!
You'll dominate mankind as if they're locusts
And starve the gods to death like Melians.

HOOP. But how?

PISTH.   Air lies between Earth and Heaven.

[151] **wedding breakfast** sesame was used for wedding-cakes and myrtle was sacred to the Goddess of Love   [159] **Teleas** the flightiest man in Athens thinks the birds flighty   [170] **economy** State   [177] **Melians** the island of Melos was starved into submission by Athens shortly before the production of this play

Just as Athenians who want to visit Pytho
180 Must get a transit visa through Boeotia
So when men offer sacrifice to Heaven
You'll stop the smoke ascending to the gods
Unless they pay a customs duty first!
    Hoop. I say! I say!
By earth, and traps, and nets, and snares, and wires,
That's the most cunning scheme I've ever heard!
I'd willingly found a city here with you
If all the other birds agree to it.
    Pisth. And who'll explain our plans to them?
    Hoop.   You can.
190 They were illiterate once, but I've been here
Living with them some time and taught them Greek.
    Pisth. How can you summon them?
    Hoop.   No trouble at all.
I'll step aside into my coppice here
And wake the nightingale. We'll call together.
They can't come fast enough to hear her voice.
    Pisth. What are you waiting for, my feathered friend?
Go straight into the coppice, I beseech you,
And wake the nightingale.

    [*The* Hoopoe *retires to sing behind the scenes*]

    Hoop. Shed your slumbers, mistress mine
200 And sound your sacred song,
With broken heart and voice divine
For Itys, my dear son and thine,
For whom we wept so long.
Trilling from your tawny throat
The sound through groves untrod
Will pass, and every blessed note
Clear as a temple bell, will float
Up to the throne of God.
Bright Phoebus with his ivory lyre
210 Will catch your voice ere long
And with accompaniment inspire
The gods to dance; and heaven's choir
Will harmonize your song.

[179] Pytho the shrine of Apollo at Delphi, the most important
oracle of ancient times

[*As the* HOOPOE *stops singing, the nightingale's voice
is heard*]

PISTH. Oh Zeus our lord and master, what a voice!
She's made the grove as sweet as honeycomb.
 EUELP. I say!
 PISTH.   What do you want?
 EUELP.   Sh!
 PISTH.   Why?
 EUELP. The hoopoe hasn't finished singing yet!
 HOOP. Whoopopo! popopopopopopoi! io, io! come,
  come, come, come!
Birds of a feather come here to me now!
Birds from the teeming fields of the country,   220
Feeding on barley and farmer's sowings,
Swift-winged, sweet-voiced, come in your thousands.
Birds that gather to follow the ploughshare,
Twittering over the upturned furrows,
Golden-tongued birds, leave your homes and come.
Tio tio tio tio tio tio tio tio.
Woodland birds building nests in the ivy
Abandon your leafy kingdoms and come.
And birds of the hills, plucking berries from branches
Of olive and arbute, fly to my call.   230
Trioto trioto totobrix.

Birds catching gnats in the olive green gorges,
Marsh birds haunting the meadows of Marathon.
Bright-feathered bird come, kingfisher come!
Sea birds skimming the swell of the ocean,
Halcyon's mates in the trough of the wave,
Come to hear what I have to say!
We summon our tribe to a grand assembly,
All the tribe of the long-necked birds.
A shrewd old fellow has come to visit us,   240
Full of invention and highly original.
Come, every one of you, come to the conference.
Come, come, come, come!

[CHORUS OF BIRDS *offstage*]

[214] **what a voice** represented by a flute offstage [230] **arbute** an
evergreen tree [233] **Marathon** on the coast, scene of the famous
defeat of the Persians in 490 B.C. [236] **Halcyon** a fabulous bird
identified with a species of kingfisher

Torotorotorotix!
Kikkabau, kikkabau!
Torotorotorotorolililix!

PISTH. Can you see any birds?

EUELP.   Apollo, no, not one.

For all my gaping up at heaven.

PISTH. The hoopoe's played the lapwing's trick, it
seems—

250 He ran away and cried and cried for nothing.

[A bird runs across the stage]

BIRD. Torotix! torotix!

PISTH. Here's one of them, old boy, at any rate!

EUELP. Zeus, yes! What is it, then? A duck-billed
platypus?

PISTH. This chap will tell us. [*Re-enter* HOOPOE] What's
that bird up there?

HOOP. None of your common-or-garden kind of birds.
That's a marsh bird.

EUELP. My word, what gorgeous flaming feathers.

HOOP. That's apt enough—we call the bird flamingo.

[Another bird enters]

EUELP. My dear fellow!

PISTH.   What are you shouting at?

EUELP.   Another one!

PISTH. You're right, by Zeus, and strangely colored,
260   too.

What wild prophetic mountain bird is that?

HOOP. His name is Turkey.

PISTH.   Turkey! Heracles!

How could a Turk get here without a camel?

[During this scene the CHORUS OF BIRDS *appear one after
another, fluttering wildly round the two travelers]*

EUELP. Here comes another in a stolen crest.

[249] **the lapwing's trick** to mislead pursuers the lapwing calls as
if to her young some distance from her real nest   [253] **duck-
billed platypus** "peacock" in the Greek; see v. 101   [261] **What
. . . that?** parody of a line from one of Aeschylus' tragedies
[262] **Turkey** in the Greek "cock," known as "the Persian bird";
here again the word must be changed to keep the joke

PISTH. What marvel's this? Aren't you the only hoopoe?
Is this your double?

HOOP. He's the son of Philocles
The Hoopoe—I'm his grandpa, as one might say
Callias begat Hipponicus and Hipponicus Callias.

PISTH. So that bird's Callias! He's lost his feathers.

HOOP. Well born but soundly plucked by bad com-
panions. 270

The women clipped his wings in next to no time!

PISTH. Poseidon, here's another gaudy fowl.
What's this one called?

HOOP. A gannet.

PISTH. What?
Is there another one besides Cleonymus?

EUELP. It can't be him, he'd throw his crest away.

PISTH. Why have they all got feathers on their heads?
Are they going to the races?

HOOP. They're like the Carians
Who build their homes on crests for safety's sake.

PISTH. Poseidon, what an ominous collection
Of birds!

EUELP. Apollo, what a swarm! Shoo, shoo! 280
You can't see the entrance for the crowds coming in.

HOOP. This one's a partridge, that by Zeus, a godwit,
Here's a duck, a halcyon over there—

PISTH. Who's that behind?

HOOP. A razorbill.

PISTH. A razorbill?

HOOP. Like Sporgilus the barber. There's an owl.

PISTH. What's this? Who's bringing owls to Athens?

HOOP. Jay, pigeon, ringdove, barn-owl, starling, lark,
Hawk, falcon, cuckoo, redshank, redcap, turtle-dove,
Flamingo, kestrel, diver, sparrow, vulture, woodpecker.

PISTH. Look at them all! Just look at all the blackbirds! 290

---

[266] **Philocles** tragic poet, presented a *"Tereus"* in 462   [268] **Callias . . . Callias** boys took their grandfather's name. Tereus'
example is an excuse for a hit at Callias, dissolute youth of a
noble family.   [274] **Cleonymus** notorious glutton and coward who
abandoned his arms at a battle   [277] **to the races** their crests re-
mind him of the helmets of men racing in armour   [286] **owls to
Athens** the owl, attribute of Athena, was so common that the
phrase became proverbial, like "coals to Newcastle"

Chattering, shrieking, and running about!

Are they fierce? Good gracious, they're opening their
  mouths

And looking us over.

  EUELP.   That's how it strikes me.

  CHORUS. Wh-wh-wh-wh-wh-wh-wh-wh-wh-where is he
  who summoned us?

In what pastures is he browsing?

  HOOP. I've long been one of you, and won't desert
  my friends.

  CHORUS. What-what-what-what-what-what-what-what
  have you to say?

What words of comfort have you for us?

  HOOP. Something for all, a gilt-edged proposition.

300 I've had some visitors, two shrewd, persuasive men.

  CHORUS. Who? Where? What did you say?

  HOOP. Two venerable gentlemen have left their people

To bring us plans of a colossal scheme.

  CHORUS. I never heard of such a thing in all my life!

What did you say?

  HOOP.   Don't let my words alarm you.

  CHORUS. What have you done?

  HOOP.   Received two travelers

Who love our life, and want to share it with us.

  CHORUS. You've done this?

  HOOP.   And very gladly too.

  CHORUS. Are they among us now?

  HOOP.   As much as I am.

310   CHORUS. Betrayed and deceived! Abandoned to shame!

Our comrade and friend has dishonored our name.

He fed in our pastures and lived at our door.

And now he's forgotten the oaths that he swore.

A faithless imposter, gone back on his words

And broken the time-honoured laws of the birds!

Brought us here by deceit to meet men, when he knows

That men are our ancient hereditary foes!

But wait! We'll have something to say to him later—

Just now we must deal with an issue much greater.

320 To punish these greybeards and put them to death.

  PISTH. We're lost!

  EUELP.   And it's all your fault, no mistake.

Why did you bring me?

PISTH.   For company's sake.

EUELP. For my tears, don't you mean?

PISTH.   Such words I despise,

For how can you weep when they've pecked out your
    eyes?

CHORUS. War! War! Bloody war!

Shoulder your wings and charge!

Get behind them and bar the door.

Don't leave them a moment at large!

Die! Die! Let's see them die

And freshen our beaks in their blood.   330

They'll find no shelter in sea or sky,

In forest or mountain or flood.

What are we waiting for? Tear them, bite them!

Where's the commander? Right flank, advance!

[*They begin to move forward*]

EUELP. That's that! Oh where can I fly?

PISTH.   No, stay!

EUELP. Stay here and let them kill you?

PISTH. And how do you reckon on getting away?

EUELP. I haven't a notion.

PISTH.   I'll tell you.

Let's stay here and fight, with these pots we're all right.

EUELP. How can a cauldron assist us?   340

PISTH. A cauldron a day keeps the barn-owl away.

I tell you they'll never resist us.

EUELP. And their sharp curly claws?

PISTH. Take that skewer of yours

And hold it in front of you, so.

EUELP. My eyes need a shield.

PISTH. This dish you must wield

Or a saucer, and watch them all go.

EUELP. My friend, you're so clever,

The best defence ever,   350

So many strategic devices!

More subtle by far in the science of war

Than Nikias with your surprises!

[*They arm themselves with the pots and pans from their
    luggage*]

[353] Nikias celebrated Athenian general, commanding the Sicilian
expedition

CHORUS. Eleleleu! Lower beaks, charge! Not a minute
    to lose! Rip, tear, cut, bite! Get the cauldron first!
HOOP. Black-hearted creatures, what are you about?
Attacking men who've done no harm at all,
And making war upon my wife's relations?
    CHORUS. Why should we spare them, any more than
    wolves?
360 Does anyone deserve our vengeance more?
    HOOP. By nature, enemies; but say by inclination
Your friends, and come to help you all—what then?
    CHORUS. How could these humans, our ancestral foes,
Be any use to us by word or deed?
    HOOP. Forewarned's forearmed—you never take advice
From friends, but from your enemies you have to.
It wasn't friends but enemies that taught
The cities to build strong walls, amass a fleet.
This knowledge saved their children, homes, possessions.
370   CHORUS. It seems to us we'd better hear them out—
Even an enemy can speak good sense.
    PISTH. They seem to be less hostile! Sound withdrawal!
    HOOP. You owe me some respect, at any rate.
    CHORUS. We've never gone against you yet in any-
    thing.
    PISTH. They're friendly, by Zeus, they're declaring a
    truce!
Ground saucepans and pot, and call it a day.
Put up your spear, we can stay inside here
And peep round the pot without going away.
    EUELP. And if we should die, who will bury us?
    PISTH.   Why,
380 We'll have six feet of earthenware, public expense!
We can say with bravado we fought at Chick-ago
To the Department for War, if we need a defence.

[They unarm themselves]

    CHORUS. Ground your hot pride, and your anger be-
    side;
Return to your places, like soldiers at arms.
We will question these two, who they are, what they do,
Before we resume our offensive alarms.
Tell us, hoopoe.
    HOOP.   Well, what would you know?

CHORUS. Who are these people, and whence do they
    come?

HOOP. From Greece they arrive, and are both much
    alive.

CHORUS. What chance brought them here to our heav-
    enly home?   390

HOOP. For your life they much care, and are anxious
    to share,

And live with you.

    CHORUS.   What do they say?

HOOP. Remarkable words, that will startle the birds.

CHORUS. Shall we reap any gain from their stay?

Will they help assist friends, or contrive our foe's ends?

    HOOP. They counsel remarkable bliss—

That you're lords of the air, up above and down there!

    CHORUS. There's something of madness in this!

    HOOP. They're wondrous wise—

CHORUS.   With a brain of great size?

HOOP. All cunning, and wisdom, and wit.   400

    CHORUS. I'm all of a flutter to hear what they utter—

Pray bid them communicate it!

    HOOP. [*To the stagehands*] Here you! Remove this
    lumber, bless it all,

And hang it in the kitchen by the fireplace.

[*They remove the pots and pans*]

Now make the speech I summoned them to hear.

Come, tell them everything.

    PISTH.   Apollo, not a word

Unless these creatures make the pledge to me

That the knife-grinder extracted from his wife—

No biting and scratching out of eyes.

    CHORUS. I pledge it.

PISTH.   Now let's hear you swear.   410

    CHORUS. I swear by this, that our play wins first prize,

By unanimous decision.

    PISTH.   That will do.

[407] **the pledge . . . wife** Panaetius, a cutler, continually fought
with his wife until they made an agreement not to hit or bite
each other   [411] **that . . . decision** the best play at the festival
was chosen by a panel of judges. Both comedy and tragedy
contain such appeals for votes.

CHORUS. And if I forfeit, by one vote alone!

HOOP. Silence in the assembly! All soldiers pile arms
and return home—watch the bulletin board for future orders.

CHORUS. Men were born to deceive, but we truly believe

That your counsel may be of some use.

We're occasionally blind, and good things slip our mind;

Perhaps you'll repair this abuse.

420 Whatever you see, impart it to me

And inform the assembly at large.

For by chance if you should have discovered some good

It will be to the general charge.

Now tell us why you came, and what you have in mind.

Don't be afraid—we won't be the first to break the truce.

PISTH. I'm blazing by Jove with a head like a stove
and a speech in the oven all hot.

I'm baker in chief—bring water, a wreath!

EUELP.   Are we going to dinner or what?

PISTH. I'm bursting with words to proclaim to the birds
of a plump and particular fashion;

Your senses will reel at the wonder you feel, so much
am I moved by compassion

To think you were kings at beginning of things—

430   HOOP.   To think we were kings? Kings of what?

PISTH. The kings of creation, the kings of our nation,
of us, Zeus in heaven, the lot!

You are older by birth and descent than the earth and
the giants and gods who protected it.

CHORUS. That's a hard one to swallow.

PISTH.   It's true by Apollo!

CHORUS.   By Zeus and I never suspected it!

PISTH. Your learning is weak, you've no curious streak,
that you've never devoured Aesop's fables,

Who says Jenny Wren was created 'ere men in his gene-
alogical tables.

---

[427] **wreath** worn by orators, but Euelpides takes it to be that
worn by banqueters [432] **giants and gods** in mythology Earth's
first inhabitants were Titans, overthrown by the gods after a
long struggle [434] **Aesop** traditionally a crippled hunchback,
author of Greek fables, possibly living about 570 B.C.

Since there was no earth at the time of her birth, when
her father took poorly and died,
She was quite at a loss where to set up his cross, and
didn't know what to decide.
She flustered and flurried, was thoroughly worried, until
at the end of a week
She buried the dead at the top of her head, interring
him there with her beak.

   EUELP. It was obvious then that the sire of the wren
had brought matters at last to a head!   440

   PISTH. If you're older by birth than the gods and the
earth then the birds should be rulers instead.

   EUELP. By Phoebus Apollo, in time that's to follow
have your beak made the sharpest you've kept her,
For Zeus he will worry and be in no hurry to see woodpecker wielding his sceptre.

   PISTH. In time prehistoric, by rule categoric, it wasn't
the gods ruled mankind,
But the birds—if you want any proof of my words, there
are plenty that leap to the mind:
First let me adduce an exemplary use, the cock, whose
power none will deny us:
So well did he work he subdued all of Turkey, 'ere anyone heard of Darius.
And such was his fame we remember his name—he is
known as the turkey-cock still!

   EUELP. You observe to this day how the cock struts
away, like a monarch imposing his will.
This brave avis rara displays his tiara erect on the top
of his head.   450

   PISTH. And such was his power from the earliest hour
that he fills us still daily with dread.
He crows without warning as soon as it's morning—each
man leaves his comfortable bed
And hurries, I vow, to workship and plough, the cobbler,
the potter, the baker,

---

⁴⁴⁶ cock see v. 262   ⁴⁴⁷ Darius the name of several kings of
Persia, notably the son of Hytaspes, who reigned from 521-485
B.C. and inspired the abortive invasion of Greece which ended
with the battle of Marathon

The tanner of hides and the bathman besides, and the
    shield-and-stringed-instrument maker.

They fasten their sandals, set light to their candles—

    EUELP.   That's true! I can say it's no joke!

It was due to the cock that I suffered a shock and was
    robbed of my Phrygian cloak

Of the finest of wool when of wine I was full having
    traveled to town for a christening.

He crowed before dinner, and I, the poor sinner, half
    asleep and not properly listening,

Assumed it was dawn, started home with a yawn; when
    I reached the town gate and went out,

I was hit till it hurt, then stripped of my shirt, and left
460   there to struggle and shout.

    PISTH. The next was the kite in monarchical right to
    take the Greeks under his wings—

    CHORUS. The Greeks?

    PISTH. It's a whim we inherit from him, the first so to
    command of our kings,

To fall flat at the sight of a hovering kite in return for
    the blessings he brings.

    EUELP. Dionysus, that's right! I spotted a kite, and
    prostrated myself on my back,

And swallowed a cent, so homeward I went with nothing
    to put in my sack.

    PISTH. The cuckoo was lord of Egypt's rich hoard; each
    year when he cuckoos again

Runs every Phoenician with great expedition to harvest
    his ripening grain.

So the birds held their sway for many a day, and in cities
    of Hellas from then on

It's the regular thing for whoever was king, Menelaus or
    Lord Agamemnon,

To have on his sceptre a bird to expect a rich gift from
470   each suitor who came.

    EUELP. I was filled with surprise, couldn't trust my
    own eyes, but then I was new to the game,

---

[456] **Phrygian cloak** of best wool, brilliantly dyed [468] **Hellas**
Greece [469] **Menelaus** King of Sparta, husband of Helen, whose
abduction began the Trojan War **Agamemnon** his brother,
king of Mycenae

When in tragedy plays Priam comes on the stage with
    a bird on his staff if you please,
Who sits through the talk with an eye like a hawk for a
    present from Lysicrates!
  PISTH. Permit me to call the best witness of all—great
    Zeus, the omnipotent King,
Who wears on his brow a great eagle even now, as
    ostensible proof of the thing,
And Athena an owl, that omniscient fowl, and Apollo
    the healer a hawk.
  EUELP. But why do they so? Please say, if you know,
    I'm mightily pleased with this talk.
  PISTH. When suppliants stand with gifts in their hand,
    as religious observance demanded,
They fly from their seat to be first at the meat, leaving
    poor Zeus empty-handed!
No one among men swore by the gods then, but every-
    one swore by the birds—   **480**
Like Lampon's "By goose!" instead of "By Zeus!" when
    he wants to go back on his words.
They revered you as god, in your footsteps they trod,
    and from you derived customs and rules,
But they treat you, I vow, very differently now,
    as ne'er-do-wells, flunkeys, and fools!
They treat you like madmen from bedlam,
Throw stones at your heads if you let them,
Bring lime to your lairs,
Wires, cages, and snares,
And come to the temples to set them!
They feel if you have any eggs,
Then hang you in clumps by the legs.   **490**
It adds to your shame
You're not even fair game,
But disposed of like offal and dregs.
They won't serve you roast, if you please
But with hot olive oil and with cheese,

[472] **Priam** King of Troy; the Trojan War was a favorite theme of
tragedy   **a bird on his staff** a sceptre, usually surmounted by
an eagle, was part of the traditional stage costume of a king
[473] **Lysicrates** either a theatrical producer or a corrupt official
suspected of bribery   [475] **who . . . now** the gods are listed
with their familiar emblems   [481] **Lampon** a soothsayer

And silphium of course,
To make a rich sauce,
And cover your carcass with these!
 CHORUS. You are free and severe in your blame.
500 We mourn our inherited powers,
So great in our forefathers' days,
So sadly depleted in ours.
Through luck you arrived at our door,
Our god-led redeemer and savior.
I'll live with you, give you my young,
In earnest of future behavior.

But now you're here, tell us what we have to do—
  life isn't worth living, if we don't try our hardest
  to get our old empire back.

 PISTH. Pay attention to my words, found one city for
510   the birds,
And don't rest until you've made an invincible blockade,
Taking extra-special care to encircle all the air
With a fence of stones and sticks, a very Babylon of
  bricks!
 EUELP. So help me, Porphyrion, a town in a million!
 PISTH. When once it's finished, your trouble's dimin-
  ished—demand the royal sceptre from Zeus,
And if he says no, and won't let it go, and seems strongly
  inclined to refuse,
Declare holy war, and lock up your door; the gods will
  soon change their demeanors
When they're kept up above and deprived of the love
  of their Semeles and their Alcmenas.
That done you must then send a herald to men to announce in appropriate words
The reversal of things, that we are now kings, they must
520   sacrifice first to the birds.
Celestial powers must yield before ours, and the gods
  must accept second sitting.

[496] silphium a herb   [514] Porphyrion one of the Titans: see vv.
432, 753, 1159   [518] their . . . Alcmenas Zeus made love to
several mortal women including Semele, who was destroyed by
lightning when he appeared before her in his full majesty, and
Alcmena, disguised as her husband

Men must first offer prayer to the fowl of the air whose
    attributes seem the most fitting.
They must offer first fruit to the white-headed coot when
    they beg Aphrodite for luck
While if they decide on a prayer to Poseidon must
    sacrifice grain to the duck.
If they should please to invoke Heracles they must give
    honey-cake to the gannet.
Whereas if they choose to kill oxen to Zeus, who rules
    our terrestrial planet,
They must sacrifice then to the birds' king, the wren, an
    entire indivisible gnat.

    EUELP. It gladdened my heart to hear the last part.
    Let Zeus go and thunder at that!

    CHORUS. What token will show we are god and not
    crow, still retaining our wings and our feathers?

    PISTH. Why Hermes, a god, with winged sandals is
    shod, and so are a lot of the others!   530
Victory flies on gold wings in the skies, and Eros the
    spirit of love.
And Hera moreover is likened by Homer to a gentle
    and timorous dove.

    EUELP. Zeus's lightning has wings, and those thunder-
    bolt things—come, hurl them all down from above!

    PISTH. Now if they are blind and dismiss us from
    mind, and keep faith with Olympus, unknowing,
Of sparrows a swarm will descend on their corn, and
    swallow their annual sowing.
And when they are starved and their income is halved,
    Demeter must issue a ration.

    EUELP. Demeter, by Zeus, is chock-full of excuses—
    she'll be in a regular passion!

    PISTH. Then crows from the skies can peck out the
    sheep's eyes and show them what sharp beaks were
    made for.
And the oxen at plough—let Apollo help now! He must
    cure them, for that's what he's paid for.

    EUELP. The oxen as well! My yoke I must sell, before
    this attack you decide on.   540

[530] **Hermes** the divine messenger, represented with winged cap,
staff and sandals   [531] **Eros** the familiar Cupid   [532] **Hera** wife of
Zeus   [536] **Demeter** the earth-goddess   [539] **Apollo** god of healing

PISTH. But if they show reverence, call you "your
eminence," Cronos, and Earth, and Poseidon,
Their life will be fair and all blessings they'll share.

HOOP. All blessings? Inform me of one!

PISTH. The locusts won't eat of the vines young and
sweet; when they see an owl-squadron they'll run!
The beetles and bugs won't get at the figs—a thrush-pla-
toon sent from above
Will pick them all off.

HOOP. But how give them wealth? For
that is their principal love.

PISTH. The birds will divine every gold-bearing mine
and show them where they're to be found
And report to the seer the best markets each year; no
sailor will ever be drowned—

HOOP. Why?

PISTH. The birds will report when the merchant who
sought information about to set off is
"Sail now, weather fair," "Storm rising, stay there"—a
meteorological office.

EUELP. My decision is made, I'll buy vessels and
550   trade—I'll come back when my fortune is found.

PISTH. They'll discover the store that in ages before
rich misers concealed in the ground,
Their silver and gold—the birds have been told! we
admit it in so many words:
"There, no one can say where it's hidden away; it's a
secret 'twixt me and the birds!"

EUELP. My ship will I sell and go dig in a well,
resurrect buried gold with my spade.

HOOP. And how shall we give them good health while
they live? Such gifts by Olympus are made.

PISTH. If a man's fat and wealthy he's sure to be
healthy; you know from your own observation
When he's in a bad way he's more sickly each day
from worry and care and starvation.

HOOP. And how to bestow a long life, do you know?
That too is a gift from Olympus.
Or must they die young?

PISTH. You have plenty among you,

---

[541] **Cronos** father of Zeus **Poseidon** god of oceans

be generous, there's no need to skimp us—
Let the birds give each man a new thirty year span.
　Hoop. But where will they get it?
　Pisth.　　　　　　　　　　From them! 560
Can it be you don't know that the rusty-voiced crow
　　outlives five generations of men?
　Euelp. They're better by far to be rulers, they are!
　　Zeus be blowed, here's my vote for the wren!
　Pisth. They'll make us better kings indeed.
To start with, they'll no temples need
Of costly stone from roof to floor
And guarded with a golden door.
In oak and hedgerow they'll recline
And olive serve them for a shrine.
To Ammon we'll not need to go
Or Delphi, but make offerings so: 570
Among the groves of arbute tree
We'll offer grain, and make our plea
With hands outstretched, for blessings sweet,
And all is ours for an ear of wheat!

　Chorus. Most sage of counselors, once our foe,
From your advice we'll never go.
So your speech has fired my heart
That willingly we'll never part.
I swear! In turn make vows to me,
Sacred, and free from villainy, 580
The gods will little longer hold
The sceptre that is mine of old.
You shall scheme and we shall fight,
Yours the cunning, ours the might!

　Hoop. By Zeus, there's no time left for nodding now!
The hour has come! Enough of wait and see!
The birds must act, and act immediately!
First step inside, to see my little nest
Of twigs and grasses, and to meet my wife—
And let me have your names!
　Pisth. 　　　　　　　Most certainly. 590
My name is Pisthetairus; this chap here,
Euelpides of Crio.

---

569 **Ammon** the oracle of Zeus Ammon in Libya　570 **Delphi see**
v. 179

HOOP.   Welcome both!
PISTH.   Thank you.
HOOP. Come inside.
PISTH.   You lead, you know the way.
HOOP.   Then follow me.
PISTH. No, wait! There's something I forgot! Come
     back again.
Look here, how can we live with you, I'd like to know,
When you have wings, and we two haven't any?
     HOOP. No trouble!
     PISTH.   But you know in Aesop's fables,
There's a story to the point, of how the fox
Lived with the eagle, and came badly off!
     HOOP. Don't be afraid—there's a root that grows up
600   here.
Just chew it. It will make your feathers sprout!
     PISTH. Then let's go in. Come Manodorus,
And Xanthias, jump to it! bring the luggage!
     CHORUS. Hoopoe, a word!
     HOOP.   What is it?
     CHORUS.   Take our friends
Inside the house and give them a good breakfast,
Then send the nightingale, the Muses' darling,
The golden-tongued, and leave her here awhile
To entertain us.
     PISTH.   Do as they ask, by Zeus.
Go fetch her from the rushes.
     EUELP.   By the immortal gods
610 Go in and call her, we should like to see her.
     HOOP. Well, if you wish, so be it! Procne!
Come out of doors, and let the strangers see you!
     PISTH. Zeus be praised, what a pretty little bird!
So delicate and fair.
     EUELP.   I'll tell you what,
I'd kiss her without any hesitation—
     PISTH. Hung over like a human girl with bracelets!
     EUELP. I will! I'll do it! I'll go and kiss her now.

---

[597] **But . . . off** the eagle and the fox decided to live together,
one at the top of the tree and the other at the foot, but when
the eagle was hungry she stole the fox's cubs for food   [602] **Man-
odorus, Xanthias** stagehands   [611] **Procne** see v. 15; represented
on the stage by a flute-player

PISTH. You fool! She's got a beak like a pair of scissors.

EUELP. By Zeus, I'll have to shell her like an egg,
Take off the covering and kiss what's underneath. 620

HOOP. Let us go.

PISTH. Lead on, and luck go with us.

[Exeunt]

CHORUS. Lovely bird of tawny throat
Precious partner of my song,
You have brought your silver note
Here to where your arts belong.
Play to us, my joy and treasure,
On your flute the songs of spring.
Strike an anapaestic measure
As the birds begin to sing.

We address mankind, who are naturally blind, and de-
cline with the fall of the leaf. 630

Frail creatures of clay that endure for a day, whose
estate is compounded of grief.

In the shadows you grope, without wings, without hope,
like dream-stuff and destined to die.

So give heed to our words, the Immortals, the Birds,
who endure for an age in the sky.

Never doomed to grow old in their heavenly fold, and
who proudly survey the Eternal.

Then listen and hear, if for truth you've an ear, of
regions sublime and infernal

The account of our birth, the creation of earth, rivers,
deities, Chaos and Hell.

When you've heard what we say you can call it a day,
and tell Prodicus go there as well!

There was Night and the Void, and Tartarus wide, and
Erebus vast and unlit,

Nor earth nor the air nor the heavens were there; then
deep in the fathomless pit

Night preened her dark wing and delivered an egg, a
wind-egg, the first of creation 640

From which at his hour blossomed Love like a flower,
awaited with anticipation,

[687] **Prodicus** a famous philosopher [638] **Tartarus** Hell **Erebus**
darkness [640] **wind-egg** wind, which alone existed, must have
been Love's father

And winged with gold feathers brought Chaos together
    with Tartarus in marital union,

From which we were born and saluted the morn; and
    instead of the previous confusion

Love made such a go of his marriage bureau he created
    a race of immortals:

Sea, heaven, and earth, and by subsequent birth the
    gods who possess heaven's portals.

From our family tree you will easily see we are seniors,
    and Love's true descendants—

We take great interest when a suit's being pressed; many
    lovers have been our dependents.

Many an obdurate heart has been softened in part by
    an opportune present of us—

It's a trick that can't fail! Give the lady a quail or a
    cock, or a parrot or goose!

Of blessings the chief we to mortals bequeath—we mark
650   winter and summer and spring.

We tell you to sow when you see the long row of mi-
    gratory cranes on the wing,

And the sailor to keep his oars dry, and sleep, and the
    thief weave a cloak good and warm.

You know from the sight of the hovering kite when it's
    sheepshearing time on the farm

And when to divest of your cloak and go dressed in a
    singlet, you know from the swallow.

We are your own Ammon, Delphi, Dodona, and we are
    your Phoebus Apollo.

You augur from birds the oracular words that determine
    the course of your lives,

Prophetic decisions on business missions, selecting your
    jobs and your wives.

And rumor can claim that it carries our name—"A little
    bird told me, I heard him!"

To be booed is "the bird" and a woman's a bird, and
    a donkey's a creature of bird-en!

Then isn't it true that we are for you your oracular
660   Phoebus Apollo?

So let us express without pausing for breath the con-
    siderable blessings that follow!

[655] **Dodona** oracular shrine of Zeus in Epirus, N.W. Greece
Phoebus Apollo also god of prophecy

[The following passage is spoken by the Leader of the
CHORUS *in one breath]*

If you greet with acclamation
Our divine self-ordination
We are free for consultation
On prophetic divination
And the seasons' circulation
And the art of orchestration!
Not like Zeus abuse our station
Hid in lofty isolation
In the nearest cloud-formation   670
But bestow our presentations
On successive generations
Of unwarlike occupations
Comic plays and recitations
With our milk for your potations
And a healthy expectation
Of long life with your relations
And your blessing—loaded nation
Bring to wealthy elevation!

Woodland muse that sings with me   680
In forest or on mountain side
As I perch in the boughs of the tall ash tree,
Your light my guide.

Tio tio tio tiotinx.

Trilling from my yellow throat
The holy hymn of praise to Pan
And the Mountain Mother's sacred note
Unknown to man.

Tio tio tio tiotinx.

Phrynichus delights to sip   690
The sweets that to my voice belong;
Lip feeds the heart, and heart the lip
With heavenly song.

Totototototototototototototinx.

[687] **Mountain Mother** Cybele, mother of the gods   [690] **Phrynichus**
early tragic poet

If any spectators wish to emulate us and spin out their
    days in high pleasure,
Come and join us up here! You have nothing to fear,
    with the birds you will have a full measure.
Whatever is banned by the law of your land and though
    pleasant is thought to be sinful,
We turn wrong into right and jet black to pure white;
    come and join us, we'll give you a skinful.
If your customs debar you from striking papa, with the
    birds it's a positive virtue;
Slap his face, say "Old cock, to your spurs you must
700   look, I regret that I'm going to hurt you!"
If a runaway slave is sufficiently brave his person to
    birdland to bring
The ignominious brand that he bears on his hand is
    "a small colored patch on the wing!"
If a Phrygian came, say Spintharus by name, in follies
    and vices a demon
We'd call him a pigeon instead of a Phrygian, of the
    honorable clan of Philemon.
Execestides, serf of low Carian birth could befeather
    his nest with relations,
And Peisias' son, the traitor, may run for protection to
    our habitation.
If he should be loth to take Loyalty Oath, we'll make
    him a cuckoo instead,
For we think nothing ill that the cuckoo should kill the
    kind parents by whom he's been fed!

> So the swans are used to sing,
710   Watching close to Hebron's banks,
> Keeping time with beat of wing,
> Their hymn of thanks.

>   Tio tio tio tiotinx.

> Ocean slumbers, breezes die,
> Forest beasts allay their fears,
> Throned upon a tranquil sky
> Apollo hears.

[708] **Spintharus, Philemon, Execestides** aliens passing themselves
off as Athenian citizens   [706] **Peisias' son** unknown; probably a
reference to some incident in the war

Tio tio tio tiotinx.

Wonder seizes heaven's lords,
Fills Olympus with amaze,   720
Muses, Graces, strike the chords,
Of hymns of praise.

Totototototototototototinx.

There's nothing like wings to get fun out of things! when
    you're bored with a play long and tragic
You can fly from your seat to get something to eat and
    be back in the benches like magic.
And conducting a shady affair with a lady who's married
    but marvellous pretty,
You could stay with her late for a sweet tête-à-tête when
    her husband's engaged in committee!
That man should wear wings is the greatest of things
    —you should ask that Dieitrephes fellow
Whose fortune was made on the wings of his trade, when
    he cornered the market in willow;
From command of platoon was promoted full soon, and
    by somewhat irregular courses   730
Is a great V.I.P. at the top of the tree, and a regular
    tawny cockhorse is!

[*Enter* PISTHETAIRUS *and* EUELPIDES, *now adorned with
wings, and the* HOOPOE]

PISTH. That's that. By Zeus this is the funniest thing
I ever saw.
    EUELP. What are you laughing at?
    PISTH. Your feathers! You know what they make you
look like?
A picture of a goose by some cheap artist.
    EUELP. And you look like a blackbird with a crewcut!
    PISTH. We're doing just what Aeschylus has said,
Winging our shafts of wit with our own feathers!
    HOOP. What's to be done?
    PISTH.   First christen our new city

---

[729] **Dieitrephes** made a fortune from wicker flasks and held high
offices in the state   [787] **what . . . said** in his lost tragedy
"*Myrmidons*"

With a big fine-sounding name, and after that
Sacrifice to the gods.

740   EUELP.   I quite agree.
HOOP. Let's see, what name would suit our city best?
EUELP. I know a good one, straight from Lacedaemon.
Let's call it Sparta. What do you think of that?
PISTH. Call our city Sparta? Heracles,
I wouldn't use esparto grass for stuffing.
EUELP. What shall we call it then?
HOOP.   A name
With local interest, something from the clouds,
Expressing emptiness.
PISTH.   Cloudcuckooland!
What about it?
HOOP.   That's a marvellous inspiration.

750   EUELP. I hereby name this state Cloudcuckooland—
The place where old Theagenes keeps his fortune,
And Aeschines his castles in the air!
PISTH. The best of all, the plain of Phlegra, where
The gods secured their victory over the Giants—so they
    say.
HOOP. What a jolly place this city is! What god
Shall we invite to be presiding deity
And take the city's present of a robe?
EUELP. What do you say to Athena Polias?
PISTH. Civic administration goes to ruin

760 With a woman driver—standing there in armour
With Cleisthenes beside her, with her knitting!
EUELP. And who'll command the citadel's stork-ade?
PISTH. The bird of Persian dynasty, the cock,
The most pugnacious bantam of them all.
EUELP. Yes, he's the fittest bird to perch on rocks.
PISTH. Now you can take a stroll around the air
And supervise construction of the walls,
And shovel stones, mix mortar in your shirt-sleeves,
And carry plates, and tumble off the ladder,

---

751 **Theagenes, Aeschines** their fortunes, much boasted of but
never seen, might be said to exist only in the clouds
753 **Phlegra** final battle between Gods and Titans   755 **What . . .
robe** Athena was presiding deity (*"Polias"*) of Athens; every
four years a richly embroidered robe was presented to her
statue   761 **Cleisthenes** an effeminate Athenian

And picket guards, and keep the fires concealed,   **770**
And challenge sentries, and fall fast asleep,
And send a herald to the gods above
And send another to mankind below
And then come back to me.

EUELP.   And you can stay
Here and be hanged for me.

PISTH.   No, friend, go where I say.
For nothing will be done if you're not there.
I'll sacrifice to our new-fangled gods.
And tell the priest lead out the procession!
Slave, bring the holy basket and the chalice.

[*The* BIRDS *begin preparations to sacrifice a goat. One of
their number acts as Priest.*]

PRIEST. I am here zealously to assist your devotions. 780
We have met together in solemn procession to glorify
the gods, and sacrifice this goat to secure their lasting
favors.

The congregation will join in the Hymn to Apollo.
[*Addressing a flute-player*] Chaeris, play!

PISTH. Stop blowing that thing! Heracles, what's this?
By Zeus, I've seen some funny things in my time,
But never a crow with a flute in his mouth!
Get on with the sacrifice, Priest, for heaven's sake.

PRIEST. The sacrifice will commence. Where is the
    ministrant? Let us pray.   790

Hearth-goddess of the birds, and the hearth-kite, and
all the birds and birdesses of Olympus—

PISTH. Hawk of Sunium, Pelargic Lord, all hail!—
PRIEST. Swan of Pytho and Delos, Leto the quail-
    mother, goldfinch Artemis—
PISTH. Goldfinch Artemis, not Colaenis Artemis—
PRIEST. Sabazian Chaffinch, and ostrich, mother of the
    gods—
PISTH. Queen Cybele, sparrow, and the mother of
    Cleocritus—   800

[785] Chaeris an unpopular piper [790] The sacrifice will commence
the following litany parodies the conventional titles of the gods
by confusing them with birds' names [800] Cleocritus an ungainly Athenian

PRIEST. Grant Cloudcuckooland health and safety for themselves and the Chians—

PISTH. I like the way the Chians get in everywhere—

PRIEST. Bird heroes and the sons of heroes, kingfisher, pelican and pelicenne, pheasant, peacock, duck, heron, sparrowhawk, blackcap, tit—

PISTH. Stop, stop, don't invoke any more! Good gracious me.

What sort of sacrifice is this for birds of prey
And vultures to assist in? Look at it!
810 Can't you see one kite could make off with the lot?
You and your garlands can get out of here—
I'll carry on the sacrifice myself.

PRIEST. Then I must use a different form of service. Hymn number two!

We praise and glorify the holy water, and summon the immortal gods—one of the immortal gods—if there's enough for even one! This sacrifice is nothing but skin and bone.

820   PISTH. Let us sacrifice, and pray to our feathered gods.

[Enter a POET]

POET.   Sing, O my Muse, in hymns of praise,
             Cloudcuckooland of happy days!

PISTH. What in the world is this? Well, who are you?

POET. The Muses' servant, working hard,

A lyric-writing, sweet-tongued bard—as Homer says!

PISTH. A servant, and you wear your hair that long?

POET. We are the Muses' busy creatures,

Mankind's self-appointed teachers—as Homer says!

PISTH. You don't work hard enough to buy new clothes!
830 Well, poet, what brings you here so soon?

POET. I have composed about your city

An epic cycle long and witty,

Gracious, charming, sure to please,

In the manner of Simonides!

PISTH. How long ago did you start on this?

POET. I've written my poetic pages

[802] **Chians** loyal allies of the Athenians and so constantly remembered in their prayers   [834] **Simonides** (556–467 B.C.) one of the most celebrated Greek lyric poets

For long, innumerable ages.

PISTH. For ages, when the town's not ten days old!
I only christened the place a minute ago.

POET. From the Muses' mouth a rumor   840
Swift as fiery horses came,
Put into your head the humor,
Etna's lord of holy fame,
To be both generous and pleasant,
Give the bard a little present!

PISTH. We've got a thundering nuisance on our hands
If we don't give him something and get rid of him.
[*He turns to one of the* CHORUS]
Here, you! You've got a shirt and tunic on—
Take it off and let the clever poet have it.
Here, take the shirt—you look as if you need it.   850

POET. My proud but not unwilling Muse
Thanks you, and does not refuse.
And now some intellectual tinder,
An apt quotation hot from Pindar.

PISTH. Confound the man! He'll never go away.

POET. In the land of the Scythian gypsies,
Strato making solitary trips is,
He says it's no joke
To have shirt but no cloak—
Can you remedy the ellipsis?   860

PISTH. I know that you want—a cloak as well!
[*To the member of the* CHORUS]
Here, off with it! We must patronize the arts.
Now take it and get out of here.

POET.   I leave you
With a valedictory ode in dialect.

> Lord on bonny sleekit throne,
> Muckle wild your winds ha' blawn.
> Through snow and storm and drumlie braes
> I ganged my wild and waefu' ways. Hoots!

[*Exit*]

---

[843] **Etna's . . . fame** parodied from an ode by Pindar to Hiero
of Syracuse: see note on v. 854   [854] **Pindar** (518-ca. 445 B.C.)
the greatest Greek lyric poet   [856] **In . . . ellipsis** parody of
another Pindaric ode

PISTH. By Zeus, he won't be cold much longer
870 Now that he's got a cloak to keep him warm.
I never anticipated such bad luck,
That he'd discover our new town so quickly.
Let's start again. Take the holy water round.
The congregation will preserve respectful silence.

[*Enter a* SOOTHSAYER]

SS. Touch not the goat!
PISTH.   Who are you?
SS.   A soothsayer!
PISTH.   Go to the devil!
SS. Rash man, don't make a joke of holy matters.
An oracle from Bakis points directly
At your Cloudcuckooland.
PISTH.   Why didn't you tell me
Before the place was founded?
SS.   God forbade me!
880 PISTH. It's precious little use to tell me now.
SS. [*Quoting from a scroll he holds in his hand*]
When wolves and hoary ravens build together
A common dwelling 'twixt Sicyon and Corinth"—
PISTH. What have the Corinthians to do with me?
SS. It's a cryptic reference by Bakis to the air

—First sacrifice to Pandora a snow white ram
And give the first prophet who expounds my words
A spotless tunic and a pair of brand-new shoes.

PISTH. Does it mention shoes as well?
SS.   Why, take the book!

If, godly youth, thou dost what I command,
890 An eagle shalt thou be in heaven; if not,
Nor eagle, dove nor woodpecker shalt thou be.

PISTH. That's what it says, is it?
SS.   Take the book!
PISTH. It's nothing like the oracle I had
From lord Apollo—I've a transcript here:

[877] **Bakis** ancient prophet   [882] **Sicyon** on the Corinthian Gulf
Corinth some miles from the modern city   [885] **Pandora** the first
created woman. Each god gave her a gift; thus she is the ideal
sponsor for the mendicant soothsayer.

If an impostor visits thee uninvited,
Disturbs thy sacrifice, and asks for meat,
Give him a tickling-up across the ribs.

SS. That's not what it says.
PISTH. [*Striking him*] Here, take the book!

And spare him not, though he be an eagle from
    heaven,
Or Lampon himself or mighty Diopeithes.   900

SS. It doesn't say that too?
PISTH.   Here, take the book!
You know the way out. Go to hell!
SS.   Oh dear!

[*Exit*]

[*Enter* METON, *with a bundle of surveying equipment*]

METON. I've come to see you.

PISTH.   Here's more trouble coming!
What are you doing? What's the big idea?
What do you want? What's all this great palaver?
    METON. I want to apportion the air into allotments
Geometrically divided.
    PISTH.   In heaven's name
What sort of man are you?
    METON.   My name is Meton
Well known in Greece and Colonus.
    PISTH.   Tell me please
What you've got there?
    METON.   Air surveying rods.   910
Now air is shaped, to take the best example,
Like a candle snuffer. I apply my ruler,
Erect my spherometrical protractors—
Do you follow me?
    PISTH.   I do not.
    METON. By applying my straight edge
I calculate the linear dimensions,

⁹⁰⁰ **Lampon . . . Diopeithes** soothsayers: see v. 481 ⁹⁰⁸ **Meton**
celebrated astronomer ⁹⁰⁹ **Colonus** district of Athens, where
Meton had constructed a water-clock

Then square the circle; where the radii intersect
We'll have your market place. The roads lead inwards
Straight to the center, something like a star
920 Which is circular, but possesses rays
Extending straight all round.

PISTH.   The man's a Thales!
I say, Meton!

METON.   Yes?

PISTH.   You know that I admire you
So take my advice and get out of my way.

METON. Why, what's the matter?

PISTH.   We're the same as Sparta—
We have witch-hunts here and frequent civic purges.
The city's full of flogging.

METON.   Revolution?

PISTH. By Zeus, not that.

METON.   What then?

PISTH.   Unanimous
Desire to whip out every charlatan.

METON. I'd better go.

PISTH.   By Zeus, I'm afraid you're too late.
930 That flogging's coming right behind you now.

METON. Oh, my unlucky stars!

PISTH.   I told you so! [*Beating him*]
Now go and measure your length somewhere outside.

[*Exit* METON. *Enter a* COMMISSIONER.]

COMMIS. Where is the Consulate?

PISTH.   The Grand Turk himself!

COMMIS. I've been allotted to Cloudcuckooland
As High Commissioner.

PISTH.   Commissioner? Who sent you?

COMMIS. Teleas' brief memorandum upon the subject.

PISTH. Would you like your salary without working
     for it?
And go back home again?

COMMIS.   I would!
I'd be able to watch my interests in the House.
940 I'm negotiating for a deal with Persia.

---

[921] **Thales** early philosopher   [933] **The Grand Turk** referring to
his pompous manner   [936] **Teleas** see v. 159

PISTH. Take it and go! This is your salary! [*Strikes him*]
COMMIS. What was that?
PISTH.   The Persian parliament.
COMMIS. You're all witnesses. A commissioner has been
  struck!
PISTH. Be off, and take your ballot-boxes with you.
This is the last straw, sending us commissioners
Before we've given sacrifice to the gods.

  [*Exit* COMMISSIONER. *Enter a* STATUTE-SELLER.]

S-S. If a citizen of Cloudcuckooland wrongs an
  Athenian—
PISTH. What's this book come to bother us?
S-S. I'm a statute-seller, come up here
To bring you new laws, at a price.
PISTH.   Such as?   950
S-S.   Cloudcuckooland shall use the weights and
                measures,
          Decrees and by-laws of the Olophyxians.
PISTH. See how you like the laws of the Asphyxians!
  [*Strikes him*]
S-S. Is something wrong?
PISTH.   Yes! Take your laws away.
You'll see some harsh laws of our own directly.
  COMMIS. I indict Pisthetairus for lese majesté at the
    coming trials!
  PISTH. Oh no, it can't be! What, are you still here?
  S-S. If anyone unseats the Government and fails to
    conduct himself in accordance with the treaty—
  PISTH. Can't I have any peace? Have you come back
    again?   960
  COMMIS. I'll win my case! Ten thousand dollars in
    damages!
  PISTH. I'll smash your ballot-boxes to smithereens.
  S-S. Do you remember committing a public nuisance?
  PISTH. Oh no! Arrest him, someone. Are you still here?
Let's go away as quickly as we can
And finish off the sacrifice inside.

                    [*Exit*]

[952] **Olophyxians** on the peninsula of Acte in N.E. Greece; the
name is introduced merely for the pun

CHORUS. Already altars burn on earth
In praise of me, the unsleeping eye,
And men invoke me in their prayers
970 As earth's immortal overseer
And guardian of the sky.

I keep the growing crops from harm
And kill the myriad insect kind
That nibble blossom on the tree
And suck the seedlings greedily
And leave the husk behind.

The garden pests that vent their spite
On bush and flower, I keep away,
And crawling things, and stinging things,
980 Whatever comes beneath my wings,
I pounce upon and slay.

But here's our special announcement for today.
A talent reward, for anyone who kills
Diagoras of Melos! And for anyone
Who kills one of the tyrants (long deceased)
A talent reward. And now we wish to read
The following: one talent for the man
Who kills Philocrates who sells the birds.
Four talents if he brings him back alive.
990 He threads dead finches on a string, and sells them
At seven for an obol—blows up thrushes
Balloon-wise, to amuse the passers-by,
Pokes little feathers up the blackbird's nostrils,
Traps doves, and keeps them prisoner to make them
Decoy their fellow birds into his nets.

That's what we have to say. If any here
Keep cage birds, we suggest that you release them
But if you don't—look out—the birds will catch you
And make you lead your friends into our nets.

[984] **Diagoras of Melos** fled from Athens to avoid prosecution for impiety, and a talent reward was offered for his capture [985] **one of the tyrants** who had seized power in Athens in the sixth century; the last was overthrown in 510 B.C.   [988] **Philocrates** see v. 13   [991] **obol** smallest Greek coin

Oh happy wingéd race of birds   1000
That never in scorching summer weather
Pant in the sun's remorseless rays
And, cloakless, face the winter days
Without an extra feather.

I make my nest in vaulted trees,
And in the flowery meadows.
And when the heat-mad crickets cry
Shrill songs of blazing noon we fly
To court the mid-day shadows.

We winter in the hollow caves   1010
And join the mountain nymphs in play,
On snow-white myrtle berries browse
And peck among the Graces' flowers
In their garden all the day.

Some advice to our judges, on where to give the prize.
Just vote for us, and all good things are yours,
Gifts richer far than those of Alexander!
First of all, what every critic sets his heart on—
The owls on silver coins will never leave you
But settle down for life inside your purses,   1020
Produce a family, and hatch small change;
On top of this, your houses will be temples.
We'll crown the gables of your roof with eagles.
If you're in State employment, wanting profit,
We'll put a little hawk into your hands
That grabs as quick as lightning; when you're dining
We'll send a crop, like ours, to store your food in.
If you vote for someone else, you'd better make
Metal head-protectors, like the statues wear.
If not, your clothes won't come home very white   1030
When the birds have done with you. We'll pay you out!

[Enter PISTHETAIRUS]

PISTH. Well, birds, the religious department's going
   splendidly.
Why isn't there a messenger from the walls
To say how things are going on up there?
Here comes someone, puffing like a grampus.

[Enter MESSENGER]

MESS. Wh-wh-wh-where's
Our general Pisthetairus?
   PISTH.   Here in person.
   MESS. The wall's completely finished!
   PISTH.   That's good news.
   MESS. The grandest, most splendid wall I've ever seen.
1040 The parapet's so large, Theagenes
And Proxenides the Bragsman, side by side,
Could drive their chariots down the width of it
Horses and all.
   PISTH.   Great Heracles!
   MESS. Its length—I calculated it myself—
A hundred fathoms.
   PISTH.   Some length, by Poseidon.
Who built this wonderful wall?
   MESS.   The birds
And no one else—no Egyptian bricklayers
Or carpenters or masons came to help us.
Our own unaided work. I was amazed!
1050 Some thirty thousand cranes arrived from Libya
Their gullets loaded with foundation stones.
The landrails dressed the masonry with beaks
And storks in millions worked as bricklayers,
While curlews and the other river birds
Brought water to the air from down below.
   PISTH. Who carried mortar for them?
   MESS.   Herons, in hods.
   PISTH. How did they lay it on?
   MESS. A most ingenious mechanical device—
The geese employed their feet as shovels,
1060 Dug deep into the hods, and slapped it on.
   PISTH. Many feet make light work.

[1040] **Theagenes** see v. 751   **Proxenides** another of the same class

MESS. And then the ducks put on their overalls
To carry bricks; and flying at their elbows
Came swallows with a shovel of cement.

PISTH. Contractors won't pay wages after this!
Come on, what's next? Who was responsible
For the wooden part of the walls?

MESS. Ingenious bird-carpenters, pelicans, who carved
  the doors
With beaks for chisels—they chopped so loud
It sounded like a shipyard hard at work.   1070
Now every entrance has its gate, the doors
Are barred, the town's perimeter guarded,
The officer's inspecting, the watchword's going round,
Patrols are out, the signal fires are ready
On every watchtower. I must run away
And have a bath. You can carry on from here.

[*Exit*]

CHORUS. What's the matter? Are you so surprised
To discover that the wall's been built already?

PISTH. I am, by heaven and surprised I may be—
I think it's an amazing feat—of lying!   1080

[*Enter* GUARD]

But here's a guard reporting from the walls
At the double, with a war-dance in his eyes.

GUARD. Help! Help! Help! Help!

PISTH. What are you shouting at?

GUARD.   Catastrophe!
One of the gods has just come down from Zeus,
Dodged past the day patrol of jack-daw guards,
Slipped through our gates, and flown into the air.

PISTH. The good-for-nothing blundering nincompoop.
What god is it?

GUARD.   We don't know—he's wearing wings.
We do know that.

PISTH.   Why didn't you send   1090
The patrol straight after him?

GUARD.   We did—
We sent thirty thousand armored cavalry, the hawks,
Advancing with their talons stripped for action.
The heavens rang with the thunder of their wings.

As they screamed through the air on the intruder's tail,
He's somewhere near, he isn't far away.

    PISTH. Why didn't you call out the catapults and
archers?

Every man parade at once—
Take aim and fire! Give me a sling, somebody!

1100   CHORUS. War is declared, unspeakable war
        Between the gods and me.
        Watch the sky where the clouds hang close,
        A god could get through, and you'd never see!
        Everyone here look well about
        At Erebus' child, the air—
        I can hear the beating of wings above us,
        There's a god flying near somewhere!

    [IRIS *descends from heaven*]

    PISTH. Here, where do you think you're going? Stand
still!

Stop fluttering about, don't move—stay where you are.
1110 Name and address! Compulsory registration!

    IRIS. My address? I'm from the gods on Mount Olympus.

    PISTH. Your name? Are you a sailing boat or bonnet?

    IRIS. Iris the fleet.

    PISTH.   What ship of the fleet?

    IRIS.   What?

    PISTH. Well, hawks, what are you waiting for? Arrest
her!

    IRIS. Me? This is an outrage! What do you mean?

    PISTH. I mean to make you suffer.

    IRIS.   The idea!

    PISTH. What gates did you enter our wall by, baggage?

    IRIS. By Zeus, I haven't an idea what gates.

    PISTH. Listen to her, she seems to think it's funny!
1120 Did you report to the jackdaw commanders, eh?

Did you apply for a pass from the storks?

    IRIS.   Impertinence!

    PISTH. Well, did you?

    IRIS.   Are you in your senses?

    PISTH.   Have you

An entrance permit issued by an officer?

[1112] **sailing boat or bonnet** referring to her flowing robes   [1113] **Iris**
rainbow-goddess, heavenly messenger

Iris. By Zeus, nobody gave me anything, my man.

Pisth. So you flew through Chaos over foreign soil,
Without reporting your arrival first?

Iris. What other way do you expect the gods to fly?

Pisth. By Zeus, don't ask me—not by that one,
     anyway.
So you're a trespasser. I suppose you know
Of all the Irises that ever were   1130
You could most justly be condemned to death?

Iris. But I'm immortal.

Pisth.   You'll die just the same.
We'd be asking for trouble, it seems to me,
If we set ourselves up as rulers, and let you gods
Carry on anyhow, never recognizing
It's your turn now to listen to your betters.
Now tell me, where are you shipping those wings of
     yours?

Iris. I'm flying down from Zeus, to tell mankind
To sacrifice to the Olympian gods,
Kill sheep, pile oxen on the altars, till   1140
The city's full of steam.

Pisth. What gods are those?

Iris. What gods, you say? Why, us, the gods in
     heaven.

Pisth. You are the gods?

Iris.   Why, are there any others?

Pisth. The birds are mankind's gods from this day
     on—
They sacrifice to them, and not to Zeus, by Zeus.

Iris. Rash man! Take care you don't provoke the
     wrath
Of heaven, or you'll feel the tooth of Zeus's vengeance
Crush your pernicious race to smithereens.
You'll have your houses burnt about your ears
By the blast of his Licymnian thunderbolts.   1150

Pisth. Listen to her! Stop talking nonsense, woman.
You think you're lecturing a crowd of natives
Who run away at tales of bogeymen?
Don't you know, if Zeus becomes too troublesome,

[1150] **Licymnian thunderbolts,** possibly referring to Euripides'
tragedy *"Licymnius"* in which someone or something was
struck by lightning

I'll send up eagles with firebrands in their beaks
To burn his palace, and the house of Amphion,
And send porphyrions dressed in leopard skins,
Six hundred odd, to hunt him out of heaven?
One Porphyrion gave him trouble enough.

IRIS. May you die with that blasphemy on your lips,
1160   my friend.

PISTH. Well, aren't you going? Hurry along! shoo, shoo!

IRIS. My father will put a stop to this impertinence.

PISTH. Oh dear, why don't you fly off somewhere else
And burn somebody who's a little younger?

[He drives her off]

CHORUS. To the godly sons of Father Zeus
            We've closed our right of way.
            No man shall send them altar smoke
            Through our city from today.

PISTH. We sent a herald with a decree to men,
1170 He should be back by now—it's strange!

[Enter HERALD]

HERALD. O Pisthetairus, blessèd and most sage,
O world renowned, most sage, most shrewd of men,
O three times blessèd—stop me can't you!

PISTH.   What do you mean?

HERALD. The people have unanimously decided
To reward your wisdom with a golden crown.

PISTH. I'll take it! How have I earned this decoration?

HERALD. O founder of our famous airy city,
Don't you know how high your reputation stands with
      men?

How many admirers you've won for this our country?
1180 Before you came to found this city here
All men were Sparta-mad—they never washed,
Or saw the barbers—dieted, had walking sticks
And played the Socrates. Now they've been converted,
Become bird-mad, and take their chief delight

[1156] **Amphion** mythical minstrel; this line, deliberately nonsensical in its present context, is taken from the *"Niobe"* by Aeschylus [1159] **Porphyrion** play on the porphyrion, a small bird, and the Titan who fought the gods: see v. 432 [1183] **played the Socrates** imitated the philosopher's eccentric habits

In imitating everything the birds do. First
They leave their beds at dawn and fly to work
As we fly off to pasture, settling down
Among the leaves—of books, and pass decrees.
They carry their infatuation on their sleeves
And lots of them adopt the names of birds.   1190
A crippled tavern-keeper's called a "partridge,"
The name of "swallow" given to Menippus,
They call Opuntius a one-eyed crow,
Philocles a lark, Theagenes a fox-goose,
Lycurgus ibis, Chaerephon a bat,
And Syracosius, magpie! Chaereas down there
Was known as quail, because he looked like one
That someone gave a wallop on the head!
They love the birds so much, they serenade them
With songs composed to swallow or to duck,   1200
Or doves, or wings, or the tiniest bit of feather.
So much for that. There's one thing I must tell you—
They're coming here, ten thousand men or more
All anxious to dress up in wings and claws.
So find wings for the immigrants from somewhere!

PISTH. By Zeus, there's no time to be standing still.
You run along as quickly as you can,
Fill boxes, baskets, hampers full of wings.
Manes can bring the wings to me outside
While I stand here to meet the applicants.   1210

[MANES, *a stagehand, brings baskets of wings*]

CHORUS.   Soon our city will be famous
          For its growing population.
PISTH. If we're lucky.
CHORUS.   Love has landed
          In our city.
PISTH.   Hurry, can't you?
CHORUS. What is there a man could wish for
          In colonial aspirations
          That our city cannot offer?
          Wisdom, Love, Ambrosia, Graces,
          Tranquil face of Peace—
PISTH.   You're idling!

1191 **A . . . head** references to contemporary Athenians, mostly
unknown   1218 **Ambrosia** food of the gods

1220 Can't you move a little faster?
    CHORUS. Bring the baskets full of feathers.
           You can start to—
    PISTH.   Beat him soundly.
    CHORUS. He's as stubborn as a donkey.
    PISTH. Manes, you're a lazy scoundrel.
    CHORUS. Put the wings in proper order,
           Wings of prophecy and music.
           Then the sea wings; you can issue
           Which appears the most appropriate.
    PISTH. By all the kestrels, you're so slow and stupid
1230 It's all I can do to keep my hands off you!

[*Enter the first of the would-be immigrants, a* SON *who
beats his father*]

    SON. [*Singing*] If I were an eagle, a high-flying eagle,
I'd leave the old country and fly to the sea—
    PISTH. It looks as though the herald told the truth—
Here's someone coming serenading eagles!
    SON. Sure, and aren't wings the sweetest thing of all?
I'm crazy with desire to be a bird.
I want to live with you—I love your laws.
    PISTH. What part of them? We birds have many laws!
    SON. I love them all—especially the one that says
1240 It's fine for birds to choke and bite their dads!
    PISTH. By Zeus, we never think a chick's grown up
Until he's tried a tussle with his father.
    SON. Sure, and isn't that the reason why I've come?
I want to break his neck, and take the property.
    PISTH. But we birds have another old commandment,
The storks preserve it in their statute tables:
    When father stork has reared his little ones
    From fledglings, and instructed them to fly,
    The chicks must care for father in their turn.
1250   SON. By Zeus, I might as well have saved my journey
If I must care for father, like the storks.
    PISTH. By no means, friend. You came with good in-
      tentions
So here's the plumage of an orphan bird.
I'm going to give you a piece of good advice—
Something I learnt myself, when I was your age!
Don't touch your father. Take the wings I give you,

These spurs in your other hand, and make believe
You've a cock's comb on your head. Join the army,
Be a soldier, and exist upon your pay.
Let your old man live—but if you're so pugnacious,   1260
Fly to the Thracian front and fight out there!
  SON. By Dionysus, I believe you're right. I'll do it.
  PISTH. It's the sensible thing, by Zeus.

      [*Exit* SON. *Enter* CINESIAS, *a minstrel.*]

  CIN. Wafted on airy pinions I soar
      To Olympian heights, meandering along
      The highways and the byways of my song—
  PISTH. This one will need a wagon-load of wings.
  CIN. —With dauntless frame, and spirit unsubdued
      To light upon fresh fields and pastures new.
  PISTH. Cinesias, the butterfly! Welcome!   1270
What brings your halting feet in this direction?
  CIN. I long to be a bird, a sweet-tongued nightingale.
  PISTH. Stop warbling, and tell me what you want.
  CIN. To have wings, to be a feather in the breeze,
To gather inspiration from the clouds
For sonnets storm-tossed on the winter wind.
  PISTH. You mean to gather sonnets from the clouds?
  CIN. Our art has its foundation in the clouds.
The gems of dithyrambic verse are here,
Poetic jewels in the twilight gleaming,   1280
High-flown, ethereal—listen, and you'll see.
  PISTH. I bet I won't.
  CIN.   By Heracles, you will.
An evocation of the air, in all its phases: [*declaiming*]

"Birds"

      Winged visions of the air
      Heaven-coursing everywhere,
      Slender-throated forms, and fair—
  PISTH. Stop!

[1261] **Thracian front** important scene of operations in the war
with Sparta [1270] **Cinesias** a talented but ungainly choral poet
[1271] **your halting feet** both his stumbling gait and the faulty
meter of his verses

CIN.   Fain would I share your airy races
1290   Riding in the wind's embraces—
PISTH. I'll wind you, by Zeus.
CIN.   Wheeling now the South to find,
          Braving now the cold North wind,
          Cleaving furrows firm and even
          In the barren tracts of Heaven.

Exquisite, don't you think? A clever thing, but mine
    own!

PISTH. [*Beating him*] Well, here's some whirling wings!
Are you happy now?
1300 CIN. Is this the way to treat a choral bard
Whose services the local choirs all fight for?

PISTH. How would you like to stay with us, and train
A choir of canaries, for Leotrophides
Of Cecrops' tribe?

CIN.   You're making fun of me,
But be assured, I shan't know any peace
Till I have wings, to fly about the air.

[*Exit*]

[*Enter an* INFORMER]

INF. Here, pretty swallow with the lovely wings,
Where are these birds that manage to live on nothing?

PISTH. Here's trouble on the prowl, and lots of it.
1310 This whining fellow's heading over here.

INF. Here, long-wings! Pretty swallow! Twice I've
    called you.

PISTH. My cloak, that's what his drunken singing
    means.
He'll need a good few swallows to cover him.

INF. Where's the man who gives out wings to new
    arrivals?

PISTH. Here at your service. What do you require?

INF. Wings, wings, that's what I want! Don't ask me
    twice.

PISTH. Do you want to fly to Pellene?

INF.   No, by Zeus.

[1303] **Leotrophides** a thin man, presumably of bird-like appearance [1304] **Cecrops' tribe** one of the tribes into which Athenian citizens were divided [1317] **Pellene** center of well-known games at which woollen cloaks were offered as prizes

I'm a summons-server on the islands,
And private eye.
    PISTH.   That's a fine profession.
    INF. And general busybody. That's why I want wings, 1320
To fly around cities laying information.
    PISTH. Would wings make business better than it is?
    INF. Impossible, by Zeus! But I'd dodge pirates
If I made the trip by air, among the cranes,
With prosecutions in my beak for ballast.
    PISTH. So that's your profession! Do you mean to say
A young fellow like you informs on strangers?
    INF. What can I lose? I don't know how to dig!
    PISTH. By Zeus, there's other more respectable work
A man like you could make his living from,   1330
By honest labor, rather than informing.
    INF. Stop preaching me a sermon, give me wings.
    PISTH. My words will give you wings.
    INF. That's stupid! How can words help me to fly?
    PISTH. Why, words give everybody wings!
    INF.   Everybody?
    PISTH. Haven't you heard the fathers talking to the
      boys
In barbers' shops like this: "Dieitrephes
Has drawn my son such airy pictures, he
Intends to be a racing driver." And another says
"That boy of mine went to a tragedy   1340
And came home so high-flown his wits flew out!"
    INF. So words can give you wings.
    PISTH.   I'm telling you.
Words elevate the human intellect
And raise man to his heights. That's why
I'm giving you the wings of good advice
To turn an honest living.
    INF.   I don't want to.
    PISTH. What will you do then?
    INF.   I'm not ashamed of my family.
My dad's old man was an informer all his life—
What's good enough for him will do for me.
Give me some wings, a lightweight racing model,   1350
A hawk's or kestrel's, so I can serve my summons
Abroad on strangers, then accuse them here,

¹³³⁷ **Dieitrephes** see v. 728; racing was a fashionable amusement

Then fly back there again.

PISTH.   I see what you're after!
You mean, you can make certain of the verdict
Before the defence arrives?

INF.   You've got it pat!

PISTH. And when he comes up here, then you fly down
To seize his goods in payment?

INF.   That's the idea
Just like a spinning top.

 PISTH.   A spinning top.
I see. Well, here's some wings for you
1360 By Zeus, the latest model from Corcyra.

[Producing a whip]

INF. So help me, it's a whip.

PISTH.   No, wings, not whip,
To whip the spinning top!

INF.   Help!

PISTH.   Fly away from here.
Drop back to earth, you gutter-scum,
You slimy, sneaking, law-perverting toad.
Take that! [*Striking him and driving him out*] Let's pack
    the wings again and go away.

[Exit]

CHORUS. We have flown on explorations,
          Seen some strange, exciting places,
          Many things we'd never heard of.
          There's a tree for instance growing
1370   Slightly to the north of Cardia—
          No one's ever seen one like it!
          Called Cleonymus, by nature
          Fat and cowardly and never
          Any use to anybody.
          In the spring it's sprouting wildly
          With a crop of accusations—
          In the winter, what a difference!
          Shedding shields instead of leafage.

[1360] **Corcyra** now Corfu, famous for its large ivory-handled
whips [1366] **We . . . leafage** the chorus interpolate a nonsense-
verse about Cleonymus, who is compared to a tree [1370] **Cardia**
in Thrace

Further on there lies a country
Near the realm of constant darkness   1380
Where you never see a candle.
Here the shades of the departed
Heroes have men-friends to breakfast
All day long except for evening.
Then you're running into danger
If you make an assignation.
If a man goes out at nightfall
He might run across Orestes.
Have his clothes stripped off, and get a
Thorough drubbing from that hero—   1390
How his right-hand side would suffer!

[*Re-enter* PISTHETAIRUS, *meeting* PROMETHEUS, *who is
muffled in a cloak and hidden under a huge umbrella*]

PROM. Oh dear, oh dear, I do hope Zeus can't see me.
Where's Pisthetairus?
    PISTH.   What on earth is this?
Who's this all muffled up?
    PROM.   Can I be watched
From heaven here? Can you see any gods?
    PISTH. Not I, by Zeus. Who are you?
    PROM.   What's the time?
    PISTH. The time of day? A little after noon.
Who are you?
    PROM.   Cow-calling time or later?
    PISTH. I've had enough of you.
    PROM.   And what's Zeus doing?
Gathering clouds or blowing them away?   1400
    PISTH. Oh go and hang yourself.
    PROM.   Then I'll unwrap.
    PISTH. My dear Prometheus!
    PROM.   Sh! Don't make such a noise.
You'll be my death if Zeus once sees me here.
I've come to tell you what's going on up there,
So take this parasol and hold it up
Above my head, and then the gods won't see me.

[1388] **Orestes** if a man visits the Underworld after dark to see the
mythical hero Orestes he might meet another Orestes, the well-
known highwayman   [1402] **Prometheus** a Titan who gave man
the gods' secret of fire, and suffered divine retribution

PISTH. I say! That's an invention like your proper self.
Unwrap yourself and speak—don't be afraid.
   PROM. Now listen to me.
   PISTH.   I'm listening, speak up.
   PROM. Zeus has had his day!
1410   PISTH.   Since when, may I ask?
   PROM. Since first you built your city in the air.
Men have stopped sacrificing to the gods
Altogether! We've not had a smell
Of altar meat from that time to this day.
It's like the Thesmophoria—we're fasting
Without our sacrifices. The barbarian gods
Are ravenous, and gibbering like Illyrians,
Threatening Zeus with a revolt in heaven
Unless he has the markets opened again
1420 For sacrificial carcasses to come through.
   PISTH. Do you have barbarian gods in heaven as well
Besides our own?
   PROM.   Barbarians there must be
Where Execestides derives his pedigree.
   PISTH. What are they called, these barbarous gods of
      yours?
   PROM. What are they called? Triballians!
   PISTH. I see—Triballians, the source of tribulation!
   PROM. That's very true. Now here's a certain tip.
A deputation's coming down from Zeus
And the Triballian gods to make a settlement
1430 For peace. Don't budge an inch, till Zeus
Yields up his sceptre to the birds, and gives
His daughter, Sovereignty, to be your wife.
   PISTH. Who is this Sovereignty?
   PROM.   A lovely girl
Who manages the thunderbolts of Zeus
And everything he has—sagacious counsel,
And law and order, wisdom, and the dockyards,
Slander, wastepaper men and ten-cent pieces.
   PISTH. She manages all this for him?
   PROM.   I tell you!

[1415] **Thesmophoria** Athenian woman's festival, with fasting on
the third day [1416] **barbarian** non-Greek [1417] **Illyrians** savages
[1423] **Execestides** see v. 11 [1425] **Triballians** a warlike tribe; Aristophanes takes their name for the belligerent barbarian gods

When once you win her from him, you'll have everything.
That's why I've come down here, to let you know.   **1440**
I've always been well-disposed towards mankind.

    PISTH. You're the only god who taught us to keep
    warm.

    PROM. I hate the gods, every one of them, you know.

    PISTH. By Zeus, I know they always hated you.

    PROM. I'm an outcast. Well, I must get back—
Here, take my parasol so Zeus can't see me
From up aloft, and I'll pretend I'm following
The basket bearer in the holy procession.

    PISTH. Then take my chair, and carry that along.

[*Exeunt*]

CHORUS. Near the Shadow-footed people   **1450**
         Lies a lake where filthy Socrat-
           es invokes the dead by magic.
         There Peisander paid a visit
         Hoping to behold the spirit
         That had vanished from his body
         With a camel-lamb to slaughter.
         There he slit the throat, departed
         Like Odysseus from the carcass.
         Up from underground directly
         To the body of the camel   **1460**
         Chaerephon the bat ascended.

[*Enter* POSEIDON, HERACLES, *and the* TRIBALLIAN, *a
deputation from the gods. The* TRIBALLIAN *clearly understands nothing of what is going on.*]

    POS. Cloudcuckooland in sight! This is the place
Our delegation's bound for. [*To the* TRIBALLIAN] You
    man there!

[1442] **who taught us to keep warm** gave man the gift of fire
[1448] **the . . . procession** an Athenian girl carried the sacred
basket in religious processions, followed by a stool-bearer
[1453] **Peisander** notorious coward   [1456] **camel-lamb** a huge lamb
[1458] **Like . . . carcass** in the "Odyssey" Odysseus sacrificed
sheep to conjure up the dead   [1461] **Chaerephon** known as "the
bat" from his night labors   [1462] **Poseidon** brother of Zeus
Heracles a demi-god, son of Zeus and Alcmena

What are you doing wearing your cloak left-handed?
Heave it over to the right-hand side like ours.
You idiot, were you born an armless wonder?
Democracy, you've brought us to a state
When gods elected such a fool as this!

TRIB. Shut up.

POS.　　　　　　　Go hang yourself! Of all the gods

1470 You're the most barbarian I've ever seen.
Well, Heracles, what's our course?

HER. I've told you—I want to break the fellow's neck
for him,

Whoever he is, for shutting off the gods.

POS. But comrade, we were sent to treat for peace!

HER. That's twice as good a reason for throttling him.

[*Enter* PISTHETAIRUS, *with some birds to roast. He pre-
tends to be busy and not to see the gods.*]

PISTH. Bring me the cheesegrater and some silphium.
Hand me the cheese—put some coal on the fire.

POS. Greeting to man from the immortal gods—
All three of us.

PISTH.　　　　I'm grating silphium.

HER. [*Greedily smelling the cooking*] What sort of
1480 meat is that?

PISTH.　　　　Some birds

Convicted of unornithological activities
Before the People's Court!

HER.　　　　　　You're grating

Siliphium on them first?

PISTH.　　　　　Why, Heracles, my friend!
What is it?

POS.　　We're ambassadors from heaven
Come to submit our armistice proposals.

PISTH. [*Still busy cooking*] The bottle's got no oil in it,
What a pity.

POS. It isn't in our interest to fight.
If you maintain a peaceful coexistence,
We offer you our rains to fill your ponds

1490 And halcyon days for perpetuity.
We have the monopoly of such concessions.

[1469] apart from a few words the Triballian speaks unintelligible
gibberish

PISTH. It wasn't us, you know, who wanted war
To start with. Now we're willing, if you like
To come to terms, providing you're prepared
To do the right thing by us—by that I mean
For Zeus to give his sceptre back again to us,
The birds. If you agree to that I now invite
The embassy to breakfast.

    HER. That's enough for me! I vote that we agree.

    Pos. What's that, you fool? Your brains are in your
      belly!   1500
Do you want to throw your father off his throne?

    PISTH. You think so? Won't the empire of the gods
Be strengthened, if the birds have power below?
As it is, men duck their heads beneath the clouds
Where you can't see them, and take your name in vain.
When once you make an alliance with the birds
If anyone swears oaths by Zeus and crow
And goes back on them, down will come the crow
Unseen, and peck out the perjurer's eyes.

    Pos. By Poseidon, there's a lot in what you say.   1510

    HER. I agree.

    Pos.   And what do you say?

    TRIB.   Er oo ar

    PISTH. You see, he thinks so too. There's something else
That we can do for your advantage. Listen:
Suppose a man has vowed to make some god
An offering, then hums and haws and says
"The gods are ever patient," and hangs on to it,
We'll deal with him.

    Pos.   And how will you do that?

    PISTH. Some moment when the man is counting out
His money, or relaxing in the bath,
A kite will swoop unseen, snatch up the price   1520
Of a pair of beasts, and take it to the gods.

    HER. I give my vote again! Let him have the sceptre
Upon those terms.

    Pos.   What does the Triballian say?

    HER. Triballian, do you want a punch on the nose?

    TRIB. Er oo sceptre oo or beating ar.

    HER. He says he agrees entirely.

    Pos. If you both agree, it's good enough for me.

    HER. Look here, we agree to the bit about the sceptre.

PISTH. By Zeus, there's something else I've just remembered—

1530 Zeus can keep Hera, as far as I'm concerned,
But he must give up Sovereignty, his daughter,
To be my wife.
    POS.   It isn't peace
You want! Let's go back home again.
    PISTH. That worries me a lot! Chef, make a good
    sweet sauce.
    HER. You fool, Poseidon, what's got into you?
Are we to go to war about one woman?
    Pos. What shall we do then?
    HER.   Why, agree, of course.
    Pos. You numskull, can't you see you're being robbed?
You're harming your own interest. If Zeus

1540 Once gives the birds his power, when he dies
You'll be a pauper. Everything he has
Comes down to you—he's left it in his will.
    PISTH. Dear me, how cunningly he's getting round
    you!
Come over here, so I can tell you something.
You have no legal claim to any part
Of Zeus's estate—you're illegitimate
And not the rightful heir.
    HER.   I'm illegitimate?
    PISTH. You are, by Zeus—his wife was not your mother!
However could Athena be his heir,

1550 A daughter, if her brothers were legitimate?
    HER. What if my father leaves me when he dies
His illegitimate profits?
    PISTH.   The law won't let him.
Poseidon, who's encouraging you now,
Will be the first to grab your father's money
On the grounds that he is the legitimate brother.
I'll tell you Solon's law upon that subject:—
    In a case where the deceased leaves legitimate issue,
    no illegitimate child shall have testatory rights. How-
    soever, if the party of the first part leaves no legiti-
1560   mate issue, the estate shall be divided equally be-
    tween the next of kin.

1556 Solon (ca. 640-559 B.C.) celebrated lawgiver and one of the Seven Sages

HER. Then I don't get a penny of the money
My father leaves?
    PISTH.   Not one, by Zeus. But tell me,
Has Zeus ever introduced you to the family?
    HER. He never has—I've often wondered why.
    PISTH. Don't stare up there with that insulted face
If you come to live with us, I'll have you made
King of the Birds, and give you milk to drink.
    HER. It seemed a fair proposal that you made
About the girl just now—I'll let you have her.   1570
    PISTH. And what do you say?
    Pos.   I vote against it.
    PISTH. The matter rests with the Triballian. Well?
    TRIB. Er oo ar pretty lass ooar big kingdom er I give
        up.
    PISTH. He says he'll give them up.
    Pos.   By Zeus he didn't.
If he did, he's only talking pidgin Greek!
    PISTH. Exactly! He says give her to the pigeons.
    Pos. You two can work it out between yourselves.
If you accept the terms, I shall abstain.
    HER. We've decided to agree to every item.
Come up yourself to heaven with us now   1580
For Sovereignty, and all there is besides.
    PISTH. Those birds were butchered just in time—
        they'll serve
For wedding breakfast.
    HER.   Shall I stay down here
And do the cooking? You can go ahead.
    PISTH. You'll roast the meat, eh? That's the glutton
        talking.
No, you come with us.
    HER.   I'd have been so happy. . . .
    PISTH. Somebody bring a tunic for my wedding. [Ex-
        eunt]
    CHORUS.   By the water-clock in Phanae
                Live a knavish people, having
                Tongues within their bellies, using   1590
                Tongues to reap the harvest, gather
                Figs and sow the corn in springtime.

1588 water-clock which timed the speeches in the law-courts
Phanae a fictitious name

And to garner in the vintage,
An uncultured set of people
Gorgias by name and Philip.
Everywhere our Attic language
Slaughtered is and mutilated
By these belly-tongue-tied Philips.

[*Enter a* HERALD]

HERALD. Bringers of fortune, mightier than speech,
1600 O three times blesséd, wingéd race of birds,
Welcome your master to his happy home
To his gold-gleaming home he comes—no star
Has ever shone so fair as he, nor sun
In all the splendor of his burning rays
Blazed half so bright, as he who now comes near
With wife whose beauty hushes human tongues,
And in his hand the wingéd spear of Zeus,
His thunderbolt; a nameless fragrance fills
The vaults of heaven, wondrous sight, and winds,
1610 Laden with incense blow the smoke away.
But he himself is come; unlock your lips
O goddess Muses, in your holy song.
     CHORUS. Forward, part ranks, flý round about to meet
          him,
The blesséd one who blessed fortune brings.
Sing, sing the shining hour and happy marriage—
Our city's god-sent savior have you been.
He brings us happy days and high endeavor
And all is prosperous where we spread our wings.
With wedding hymn and bridal chorus greet him
1620 Our bridegroom Pisthetairus and his queen.

[*Enter* PISTHETAIRUS *and* SOVEREIGNTY]

To Hera on Olympus' height
The Fates conducted Heaven's lord
From lofty throne, and at their rite,
Sung out this hymn in one accord:

[1598] **By . . . Philips** Greek is mutilated by foreign orators and
philosophers now filling the schools and law-courts of Athens

      O Hymen, Hymenaeus, O
      O Hymen, Hymenaeus.
    Love that makes all things to grow
    Attended at their marriage bed,
    Gave rein to their desires, and so
    Were Zeus and happy Hera wed.   1630
      O Hymen, Hymenaeus, O
      O Hymen, Hymenaeus.

PISTH. I love your wedding hymns and love your songs
And revel in your words. So come take now
The infernal thunder that to Zeus belongs
And lock the blazing lightning up below.
This too, the thunderbolt that terrifies,
The fiery-tailed destroyer from the skies.

    CHORUS.   Awful golden lightning flash,
              God's immortal fiery spear,   1640
              Thunder that with hellish clash
              Makes rain torrents to appear.
              By the power that lies in this
              He may shake both land and sea.
              Zeus's empire, all is his,
              And his handmaid, Sovereignty.

PISTH. Follow in my wedding train
Feathered friends whose life I shared,
To the resting place of Zeus
And my happy marriage bed.   1650
Come blesséd wife give me your hand,
Rest it here upon my feathers,
Rise into the air with me,
Let us dance through life together.

    CHORUS.   A hymn of praise, Alleluiah!
              All hail, most mighty conqueror
              The greatest god of all.

[1625] **Hymen, Hymenaeus** names of the god of marriage

DRAMATIS PERSONAE

❧

SPONGE, a Parasite
MENAECHMUS, a citizen of Epidamnus
MENAECHMUS, once called Sosicles, of Syracuse
EROTIUM, a woman of ill-repute
CYLINDRUS, her cook
MESSENIO, slave to Menaechmus of Syracuse
WIFE of MENAECHMUS of EPIDAMNUS
Her Father
A Doctor
A Maid

Sailors, Slaves

SCENE: *A street in Epidamnus.*[1] *On one side the house of* MENAECHMUS, *on the other, that of* EROTIUM.

Titus Maccius Plautus

THE BROTHERS MENAECHMUS

❧

Act I

[*Enter* SPONGE. *He advances to the front of the stage and addresses the audience.*]

SPONGE. My name is Sponge—so called by my young friends, because I always soak up what's on the table. If you ask me, men are great fools to chain up their prisoners, or clap runaway slaves in irons. When a man's in a bad way, and one trouble comes on top of another, he's the more eager to do wrong and run away. They slip their chains somehow—file through their fetters, or smash the padlock with a stone, and think nothing of it. If there's someone you want to keep safe, and make sure he won't run away, bind him to you with food and drink. Set a good table and strap his snout to that. As long as you wine and dine him every day at his pleasure, till he's had enough, escape won't enter his head, even if he's condemned to death. You'll keep him easily, as long as you use chains like that. The stomach's a chain that never lets go—the more you stretch it, the tighter it holds you. Take me; I'm paying Menaechmus a visit. I've been his property[2] for years, and go willingly to have my chains put on. He doesn't simply feed men, oh no! It's an education, a new lease of life to dine with him. He's the best doctor in the world. That's the sort of young man he is—he has a colossal appetite himself, and gives banquets fit for the gods—loads the tables, piles the plates so high you have to stand on

---

[1] **Epidamnus** now Durazzo on the Illyrian coast opposite Brindisi [2] **his property** a humorous reference to the Roman law whereby the creditor could imprison his debtor until the debt was worked out

your chair to reach the top. It's many days since I saw him last—no invitation! I've been at home with my dear ones—everything I eat or buy comes very dear indeed! But now my supply corps has deserted, I'm paying him a visit. His door's opening! [3] Look, Menaechmus in person! He's coming outside.

[MENAECHMUS *of* EPIDAMNUS *emerges from his house angrily addressing his wife who remains inside. He does not see* SPONGE. *Under his cloak he wears a woman's gown.*]

MEN. If you weren't so stupid and obstinate, if you could only control yourself, you'd never do what you can see your husband dislikes. And another thing—if you ever behave this way again, I'll divorce you and send you back to your father.[4] Every time I want to leave the house, you call me back, keep me waiting, ask me questions: Where am I going? What am I doing? What's my business? What am I going out for? What have I got with me? What am I taking from the house? I've married a customs officer, not a wife. I have to give an account of all my business, all I've done and all I'm doing. I've spoiled you. Right! I'll tell you what I'm going to do. Since I'm the one who feeds you, gives you servants, jewels, fine clothes, wool to spin, and sees that you don't want for a single thing, look out for squalls if you've any sense—stop watching your husband. But you've taken a lot of trouble, so I'll give you something to watch for; I'll take my mistress and go out to dinner.

SPONGE. [*Aside*] This man may think he's cursing his wife, but he's cursing me—if he dines out, he's punishing me, not her.

MEN. Phew! At last! I've driven her inside—she couldn't stand the rough edge of my tongue. Where are you, husbands who keep mistresses? What are you waiting for? Where are your bouquets and congratulations? I've fought well for the cause! This gown is my wife's; I've sneaked it out of the house to take to my mistress.

[3] **His door's opening** used frequently in Roman comedy to fix the attention of the audience on a coming entrance　[4] **back to your father** by Roman law a man could divorce his wife by sending her away and restoring her dowry

That's a fine way to cheat my jailer, the old hawk. A rare theft, a merry theft, an honest theft—and carried out like a professional. Stolen from a shrew—a shrewd blow to my pocket, but my mistress shall have it. I've plundered the enemy, and my friends shall have the spoils.

SPONGE. Ahem! My young friend; is there a cut for me?

MEN. I'm done for, I've fallen among thieves.

SPONGE. No, no, among allies. Don't be afraid.

MEN. Who is it?

SPONGE. Me.

MEN. Opportunity in person, old Nick of time. Good day to you.

SPONGE. And to you.

MEN. How's things?

SPONGE. I grasp my guardian angel by the hand.

MEN. You couldn't have appeared at a better moment.

SPONGE. A habit of mine—I'm always punctual to my own advantage.

MEN. Do you want to see something really worth seeing?

SPONGE. Who cooked it? [5] Just let me see the peelings, and I'll tell you if it's all right.

MEN. Tell me, have you ever seen that wall painting of the eagle carrying off Ganymede, or Venus with Adonis? [6]

SPONGE. Often; but what have they to do with me?

MEN. Take a look at me. See any resemblance?

[SPONGE *sees the gown*]

SPONGE. What's all this fancy goods?

MEN. Say I'm the wittiest man you ever saw.

SPONGE. Where are we eating?

MEN. Just say what you're told.

SPONGE. All right; you're the wittiest man I ever saw.

MEN. Any spontaneous comment you'd care to add?

SPONGE. And the jolliest.

MEN. More, more.

---

[5] **Who cooked it?** his mind immediately turns to food   [6] **Ganymede** a youth carried off to heaven by an eagle to be the cup-bearer of Zeus, **Adonis** stolen when a baby by Venus. Menaechmus compares his own theft to these well-known stories.

SPONGE. No more till I know why. You're quarrelling with your wife—I'm going carefully where you're concerned.

MEN. Don't worry; if we can't get in at home, there's another place where we can be on our own, and bury my wife and the day together.

SPONGE. Fair enough! How soon can I start the cremation? The day's half dead to the waist already.

MEN. You're keeping me waiting with this talk.

SPONGE. You may knock out my eye, Menaechmus, if I say another word without being told.

MEN. Come over here, away from my door.

SPONGE. All right.

MEN. Over here a bit more.

SPONGE. As you like.

MEN. Further, further—don't be afraid; get away from that lion's den.

SPONGE. My word, I should say you'd make a good racing-driver.

MEN. Why?

SPONGE. You keep looking back to see if your wife's after you!

MEN. Now what do you say—

SPONGE. What do I say? Yes, no, whatever you want me to say!

MEN. Come on, smell this gown I've got here. What does it smell of?

SPONGE. It smells of theft; it smells of mistress; it smells of dinner.

MEN. Now let's take it to my lady-love Erotium. I'll tell her to prepare dinner for me, you and herself, and we'll drink till the rising of the morning star.

SPONGE. You couldn't put it plainer. Shall I knock?

MEN. Yes, knock—no, wait a minute.

SPONGE. The cup was at my lips—now it's a mile away.

MEN. Knock gently.

SPONGE. You must be afraid the door's made of china.[7]

---

[7] **china** literally "Samian," a delicate pottery which later became very popular

MEN. Wait, wait, for heaven's sake. She's coming out!
Look at the sun! it's eclipsed beside her beauty! What
more do you want?

[*Enter* EROTIUM *from her house*]

EROT. Menaechmus, my heart's delight, I'm glad to
see you!

SPONGE. What about me?

EROT. You aren't one of my gentlemen.

SPONGE. Every regiment has its camp followers.

MEN. I should like to order battle to be prepared
today, between my friend and myself, at your house.

EROT. Today it shall be.

MEN. The two of us will have a drinking match; and
the one who shows more valor in his cups is yours. You
shall be judge, and decide in whose arms you'll spend
the night. Oh my little pet, when I look at you, how I
detest my wife.

EROT. That may be, but you still have to dress up
in her wardrobe. What's this?

MEN. Her loss and your gain, my rosebud.

EROT. The winner! You're far more of a gentleman
than any of my other callers.

SPONGE. A harlot's full of caresses when she sees
something she'd like to get her hands on. If you really
loved him, you should have bitten off his nose by this
time!

[MENAECHMUS *takes off his cloak, showing his wife's
gown underneath*]

MEN. Take this, Sponge; I want to make the offering
I promised.

SPONGE. Right you are; but do me a favor, give us
a dance[8] while you're wearing it.

MEN. Dance? Me? You're mad.

SPONGE. Which of us is the madder, I wonder? Well,
if you won't dance, take it off.

MEN. I stole this today at tremendous risk. If you ask
me, Hercules never went through such danger to steal

[8] **a dance** like the effeminate dancers who performed in
women's costume

Hippolyta's girdle.[9] Take it; you're the only person who really understands me.

EROT. That's how an honest lover should behave.

SPONGE. [Aside] If he wants to end up in the gutter.

MEN. I gave four minae[10] for it for my wife a year ago.

SPONGE. [Aside] I make that four minae down the drain.

MEN. You know what I want you to do for me?

EROT. I know, I'll do what you want.

MEN. Then have dinner ready for the three of us at your place, and get something special from the market—sucking-pig with chestnut stuffing or a smoked ham, or a boar's head or something like that, that will fill me up when it's cooked—I'm as hungry as a hawk. And be quick about it!

EROT. Just as you say.

MEN. We'll go down to the Forum[11] and be back directly. We can have a drink while it's cooking.

EROT. Come when you like; everything will be ready.

MEN. Just be quick then. Come along you.

SPONGE. I'm at your service, right behind you. I wouldn't lose you today for all the riches of Heaven.

[Exeunt MENAECHMUS and SPONGE to the Forum. EROTIUM steps back to her house and calls inside.]

EROT. Call Cylindrus my cook out here to me, and look sharp.

[Enter CYLINDRUS]

Take a basket and money. Here's three nummi.[12]

CYL. I've got them.

EROT. Go and get food. See there's enough for three—not too little, not too much either.

CYL. What sort of guests are coming?

EROT. Myself, Menaechmus and his parasite.

CYL. That's ten already—the parasite can eat enough for eight.

[9] **Hippolyta's girdle** as his ninth labor Hercules was ordered to steal the girdle of Hippolyta, Queen of the Amazons, and had to fight the warrior women for it   [10] **minae** the mina was a Greek coin   [11] **Forum** market-square and place of assembly   [12] **nummi** general word for "coins" but here probably Greek silver pieces

EROT. I've told you who's coming—you see to the rest.

CYL. Very well. Dinner is as good as served. Tell them to be seated.

EROT. Hurry back.

CYL. I'm here already.

[*Exeunt* EROTIUM *to the house and* CYLINDRUS *to the market*]

Act II

[*Enter* MENAECHMUS *of* SYRACUSE, MESSENIO, *and sailors with baggage*]

MEN. S. If you ask me, Messenio, a sailor's greatest pleasure is the first, distant sight of land.

MESS. Not to deceive you, sir, it's more pleasant still if the land happens to be the one you were born in. But tell me why you've come to Epidamnus? And why we've gone round every island, just like the sea?

MEN. S. To look for my twin brother.

MESS. Then how much longer are we going to look for him? Six years it is now, since we started; we've been to the Danube, Spain, the South of France, Illyria, the Greek colonies[1] and the whole coast of Italy wherever the sea can reach. If you'd been looking for a needle I should think you'd have found it long ago, if there was one. We're looking for a dead man among the living. We should have found him years ago, if he were still alive.

MEN. S. Then I want to make sure, by finding someone who can say he knows he's dead. After that I won't trouble to search any more. If not, I'll never give up the hunt while he's alive. I know how dear he is to my heart.

MESS. You're looking for a needle in a haystack. Why don't we go home—unless we mean to write a travel book?

MEN. S. Stop being clever, unless you want trouble. Don't interfere—I'll do this thing my way.

[1] the Greek colonies in Sicily and Southern Italy

MESS. That teaches me that I'm a slave. He couldn't put more meaning into fewer words. No, I can't help it, I must speak. Listen to me, Menaechmus. To look at our purse, we're only out for a summer excursion. If you ask me, unless you go home you'll be in no end of bother looking for your brother when everything's gone. As for the people that live here! Epidamnus is where all the gay sparks and heavy drinkers come from; this is where the sharpers live, and the confidence men; and they say the harlots here are more seductive than anywhere else on earth. That's why it's called Epidamnus—because you're damned as soon as you set foot in the place.

MEN. S. I'll look out for that. Give me the purse.

MESS. Why do you want it?

MEN. S. I'm worried by what you said.

MESS. What about?

MEN. S. That you'll prove my damnation here in Epidamnus. You're a great one for the girls, Messenio, and I'm very apt to lose my temper, I can't control myself. So if I keep the money, I'll guard against both things—that you don't steal it, and that I don't fly into a rage with you.

MESS. Take it and keep it. A pleasure, I'm sure.

[Enter CYLINDRUS from the market]

CYL. I've done a good day's shopping if you ask me—a fine dinner to set before the guests. But there's Menaechmus[2] before my very eyes. Oh, my back will feel this! Guests strolling round the front door before I've finished shopping. I'll go and speak to him. Good-day, Menaechmus.

MEN. S. God bless you, whoever you are. [*To* MESSENIO] Do you know who this is? He knows who I am.

MESS. Blowed if I do.

CYL. Where are the other guests?

MEN. S. What guests are you looking for?

CYL. Your parasite.

MEN. S. My parasite? This fellow's out of his mind.

[2] But there's Menaechmus Cylindrus takes one twin for the other, thus setting off the train of misunderstandings

MESS. Didn't I tell you this place was full of blood-suckers?

MEN. S. Who's this parasite of mine you're looking for?

CYL. Sponge.

MEN. S. What Sponge? And how mine?

MESS. I've got your sponge safe here in the kitbag.

CYL. You're too early for dinner, Menaechmus, I'm just back from shopping.

MEN. S. Tell me, boy; how much do pigs for sacrifice cost here?

CYL. One nummus.

MEN. S. Then take it—get yourself absolved [3] at my expense. You must be mad, I'm sure, to trouble a stranger like myself, whoever you are.

CYL. Your name's Menaechmus, at least as far as I know.

MEN. S. You're talking sanely enough when you use my name. Where did you get to know me?

CYL. Where did I get to know you? When you're keeping my mistress Erotium here?

MEN. S. I'm not keeping her, and I don't know you.

CYL. I'm Cylindrus; don't you know my name?

MEN. S. Cylindrus or Coriendrus,[4] you can go to the devil. I don't know you, and I don't want to.

CYL. Don't know me? After all the times I've filled your cup at our place?

MESS. If only I had something to split his head open!

MEN. S. You're used to filling my cup—when I've never been to Epidamnus or set eyes upon it before today?

CYL. You haven't?

MEN. S. I certainly haven't.

CYL. You don't live in that house?

MEN. S. Devil take the people who live in that house.

CYL. He's mad, all right, when he curses himself. I say, Menaechmus!

MEN. S. Well?

[3] **Get yourself absolved** insanity was regarded as a divine afflic-tion, so sacrificing to the gods might lead to a cure. A pig was commonly used for such purposes. [4] **Coriendrus** from cori-andrum, a seed used as cake-flavoring

CYL. That nummus you just promised me—if you take my advice, have a piglet sacrificed on your own behalf, if you have any sense.

MEN. S. Heavens above, what a dreadful nuisance this man is.

CYL. He likes to have his little joke with me—as witty as you please, when his wife's not about. I say!

MEN. S. What do you want, you rascal?

CYL. Look here! Have I bought enough for the three of you—you, the lady, and your parasite—or shall I get more?

MEN. S. What lady? What parasite? What are you talking about?

MESS. What are you up to, pestering him like this?

CYL. What business is it of yours? I don't know you. I'm addressing this gentleman, I know him.

MESS. You're mad all right, I know that.

CYL. They'll be cooking directly, trust me. You won't have to wait. Don't go too far from the house. Anything else you want?

MEN. S. For you to go to perdition.

CYL. Better if you went—inside and sat down, while I set these before the violence of Vulcan.[5] I'll go in and tell Erotium you're here, then she can take you inside, instead of letting you hang round the door.

[CYLINDRUS *takes the meat into the house*]

MEN. S. Has he gone? Yes. Now I know you were telling the truth.

MESS. Watch out, that's all. If you ask me the lady of the house is no better than she ought to be—as that lunatic said who just went in.

MEN. S. And yet I'm astonished he should know my name.

MESS. That's no wonder. It's what these women always do—send their maids and potboys round to the harbor whenever a foreign ship comes in, to ask the captain's name and where he comes from. Then they hang round him like flies and when they've got him interested carry

[5] **Vulcan** the smith-god; hence fire was his province. A deliberately pompous phrase put into the slave's mouth for comic effect.

him off to the brothel. There's a pirate ship waiting in
that harbor⁶; we'd better steer clear of it, if you ask me.

MEN. S. That's good advice.

MESS. I'd know it was, if you took it.

MEN. S. Quiet a minute. The door banged. Let's see
who comes out.

MESS. I'll drop these while we wait.

[*He puts down the baggage he is carrying*]

Watch it, my hearties!

[EROTIUM *emerges from her house, giving instructions
to a maid*]

EROT. Leave the door as it is—get in, I don't want
it shut. Take care everything's ready inside—see the
needful's done. Spread some cushions, burn perfume.
The customers like to have things clean. It makes them
spend, but it's good for us! Where is he? My cook said
he was outside. I see him—my biggest source of income, my gold mine. He deserves to have first say in
my house. I'll go and speak to him. Sweetheart, I can't
believe my eyes to see you standing out there—the
door's never shut to you; this house is more your own
than yours is. Everything you ordered is ready, just
as you wanted, and there's nothing to keep you waiting
outside. Here's dinner ready, as you ordered—take your
seat when you like.

MEN. S. Who's this woman talking to?

EROT. You, of course.

MEN. S. What have I now or ever had to do with you?

EROT. Because the Goddess of Love desired me, out
of all my gentlemen, to make much of you. And it's no
more than you deserve—it's you and your kindness alone
that have set me up so well.

MEN. S. This woman must be either mad or drunk,
Messenio, to be so familiar with a complete stranger.

MESS. Didn't I tell you what went on here? This is
just the falling of the leaves—if we're still here in
three days' time, you'll have whole tree trunks on your
head. That's what the harlots are like here, all after

⁶ **a pirate ship** he speaks metaphorically, meaning Erotium

your money. Let me tackle her. Now listen, woman, I'm talking to you.

EROT. Well?

MESS. Where did you meet this man?

EROT. The same place where he met me a good many times—in Epidamnus.

MESS. In Epidamnus? When he hasn't set foot in the place before today?

EROT. Oh, you're joking. Menaechmus mine, please come in—it's nicer inside.

MEN. S. This woman's got my name off pat—this is a fantastic business.

MESS. She's smelt the purse you're carrying.

MEN. S. A timely warning. Take it. Now I'll know if it's me she loves or my money.

EROT. Let's go in and have dinner.

MEN. S. Kind of you to ask me, but I'm afraid I must refuse.

EROT. Then why did you tell me to cook dinner for you just now?

MEN. S. I told you to cook dinner?

EROT. Yes, for you and your parasite.

MEN. S. What parasite, damn him? She must be mad.

EROT. Sponge.

MEN. S. What sponge? to clean shoes with?

EROT. The one who came with you before, when you brought me that gown you'd stolen from your wife.

MEN. S. What! I gave you a gown I'd stolen from my wife? Are you mad? She must be asleep on her feet like a horse.

EROT. Why do you laugh at me like that and deny the truth?

MEN. S. Tell me what I've said I didn't do that I did.

EROT. Gave me your wife's gown this very day.

MEN. S. I did no such thing. I never had a wife, and haven't one now. I've never crossed your threshhold since the day I was born. I had breakfast on the ship, then came ashore and met you here.

EROT. Oh, I can't stand any more of this. What ship are you talking about now?

MEN. S. A wooden one—had a few knocks, sprung a

few leaks, had a few bangs with the mallet. It's got as many pegs in it as a fur shop.

EROT. No more fooling, there's a dear, come along with me.

MEN. S. You're looking for some other man, my dear, not me.

EROT. Don't I know you? Menaechmus, son of Moschus, born in Sicily at Syracuse, so they say? Where Agathocles[7] was King, then Phintia, then Liparo, who left the kingdom to Hiero on his death, who's ruling now?

MEN. S. There's not a word of untruth in that.

MESS. By Jupiter, has she ever been to Sicily to know you so well?

MEN. S. I don't see how I can refuse her.

MESS. Don't do it! cross that threshold and you're lost.

MEN. S. Be quiet—everything's all right. I'll agree to whatever she says, if I can get a meal out of it. [To EROTIUM] I deliberately contradicted you before, my dear—I was afraid this fellow might tell my wife about the gown and our dinner. Now let's go in when you like.

EROT. Are you waiting for your parasite?

MEN. S. I'm not, and I don't give a hang for him. If he comes I don't want him let in.

EROT. I'll do that with pleasure. Guess what I'd like you to do for me?

MEN. S. You only have to tell me.

EROT. Take the gown you just gave me to the embroiderer's to be remade, and have some trimmings I'd like added.

MEN. S. How right you are. That will disguise it, and my wife won't know you've got it if she sees it in the street.

EROT. Take it with you, then, when you go.

MEN. S. A pleasure.

---

[7] **Agathocles** her history is inaccurate. Agathocles reigned from 317 to 289 B.C., and Hiero gained power by force in 265, ruling until 215. Phintia was tyrant not of Syracuse but of Agrigentum, and Liparo seems to be a fictitious name.

Erot. Let's go in.

Men. S. Go ahead, I'll follow you. I want to have a word with this fellow. Pssst! Messenio! Here!

Mess. What's up?

Men. S. Pick up the luggage.

Mess. Why?

Men. S. Because you must. I know what you're going to say.

Mess. So much the worse for you, then.

Men. S. I've got my hands on the spoils, the siege has begun. Take your mates to an inn directly, and see you're back to meet me before sunset.

Mess. Don't you know what a harlot is, master?

Men. S. Quiet, I tell you, go away. If I make a fool of myself I'll suffer for it, not you. This woman's a fool, she doesn't know what she's doing. As far as I could see, there are pickings here for us.

[*Exit into* Erotium's *house*]

Mess. And that's the end of me. Off already? That's the end of him. He's steering his rowboat straight for the pirate galleon. But I'm the fool for thinking I could control my master. He bought me to listen to him, not to tell him what to do. Follow me—then I can do as I'm told, and come to meet him in time.

[*Exit* Messenio, *followed by the sailors with the luggage*]

Act III

[Enter Sponge *from the Forum*]

Sponge. In all my thirty years, I've never done anything sillier or more criminal than today, when I got myself involved in a meeting. While I sat yawning there, Menaechmus gave me the slip, and went off to his lady friend, I suppose, and didn't want my company. Damnation on the man who invented meetings, to take up men's time when they're busy enough already. It's no occupation for men of leisure. There are plenty of men who only eat once a day, and have nothing to do— who neither get invitations nor give them. They're the ones who ought to join meetings and committees. If things were run that way I shouldn't have lost today's dinner. I feel more like a corpse than a human being. Well, I'll go along—it's some comfort even to think of the scraps. What's this?

[*Enter* MENAECHMUS *of* SYRACUSE, *drunk, with a wreath in his hair, from* EROTIUM's *house*]

Menaechmus? Coming out with a wreath on his head? They've cleared away, and I'm just in time to take him home. I'll watch what he's up to, and then go and speak to him.

MEN. S. [*Talking to* EROTIUM *inside the house. He has the gown with him.*] Will it keep you quiet if I have some clever alterations made and bring it back some time today? I promise you won't know it's the same, you'll never recognise it.

SPONGE. He's full, he's talking about me and what I've missed. Dinner's over, the wine's drunk, the parasite's been shut out, and now he's taking the dress to the embroiderer. I'm not the man I think I am, if I don't pay him out for wronging me. See what I'll give him!

MEN. S. Almighty gods, what man ever hoped less for your favors and enjoyed them more in one day? I've had food, drink, and love—and stolen this gown, which no one will ever be able to claim after today!

SPONGE. I can't hear what he's saying if I stay in hiding.

MEN. S. She says I stole it from my wife to give to her. As soon as I saw her mistake, I began agreeing with her, as if we really were acquainted. Whatever she said, I said. So to cut a long story short, I was never better off in my life at less expense.

SPONGE. I'll approach him—I'm longing for a fight.

MEN. S. Who's this coming towards me?

SPONGE. What have you to say for yourself? You cheat, you shyster, you feather in the wind, you despicable, worthless thief! What have I ever done to you, for you to ruin me? Why did you sneak away from the Forum earlier on, and put paid to dinner when I wasn't there? How could you dare? It was mine as much as yours.

MEN. S. What do you want with me, young fellow? Coming here on purpose to insult a complete stranger! Do you want your hard words paid back in hard knocks?

SPONGE. You've given me a hard knock already, I know that.

MEN. S. What's your name, young man? Speak up!

SPONGE. Are you trying to make a fool of me, pretending not to know my name?

MEN. S. To the best of my knowledge I never met you or set eyes on you before today. Play fair, whoever you are; stop making a nuisance of yourself.

SPONGE. You don't know me?

MEN. S. I wouldn't say I didn't if I did.

SPONGE. Wake up, Menaechmus.

MEN. S. I am awake, as far as I know.

SPONGE. Don't you know your parasite?

MEN. S. You're not quite right in the head, young man, that's all I know.

SPONGE. Tell me, did you not steal that gown from your wife today, and give it to Erotium?

MEN. S. I don't have a wife, I didn't give it to Erotium, I never stole any gown.

SPONGE. Are you mad? There's nothing more to be got out of him. Didn't I see you go out in your wife's gown?

MEN. S. Confound you! Do you think all men as effeminate as you are? You say I was wearing a woman's gown?

SPONGE. I do.

MEN. S. Be off where you belong and get someone to pray for you, you lunatic.

SPONGE. I don't care who tries to stop me—I'm going straight to your wife with the whole story. You'll never hear the end of this. I'll teach you to eat my dinner.

[*Exit to* MENAECHMUS' *house*]

MEN. S. What's all this about? Everyone I see seems to be having a game with me. Hullo, the door opened.

[*Enter* EROTIUM'S MAID *from the house*]

MAID. Menaechmus, here's a message from Erotium—she'd be very glad if you took this to the jeweller's at

WIFE. You're talking nonsense.

MEN. It is one of the servants you're angry with, isn't it?

WIFE. Nonsense!

MEN. You can't be angry with me?

WIFE. You're talking sense at last.

MEN. But I've done nothing wrong.

WIFE. Nonsense again!

MEN. What is this, wife?

WIFE. Are you asking me?

MEN. Would you rather I asked him? What's up?

WIFE. Gown.

MEN. Gown? Why do you say gown?

SPONGE. What are you frowning at?

MEN. I'm not. [*Aside*] Only at one thing—the gown makes me frown.

SPONGE. I'll teach you to eat up my dinner when my back was turned. [*To the* WIFE] Keep at him.

MEN. Be quiet.

SPONGE. I won't. He's shaking his head at me not to speak.

MEN. Well! I never shook my head, or winked at you.

SPONGE. Did you ever see more assurance? Denying the obvious!

MEN. Wife, I swear by Jupiter and all the gods—are you satisfied?—that I didn't do it.

SPONGE. All right, she believes you; now get back to the point.

MEN. Get back to where?

SPONGE. To the embroiderer, I should think—get the gown back!

MEN. What gown?

SPONGE. I'm not saying another word, when he can't remember his own actions.

WIFE. Did you think you could do a thing like that and get away with it? You took it with interest! And you'll pay it, too.

SPONGE. Yes, you'll pay it too. Go on, eat my dinner without me; go on, get drunk, put flowers in your hair, make a fool of me outside the house.

MEN. I haven't had dinner—I haven't put my foot inside the door today.

the same time, add an ounce of gold to it and have a new bracelet made.

MEN. S. This and anything else she wants done. Tell her I'll do what she likes.

MAID. Do you know which bracelet this is?

MEN. S. All I know is it's a gold one.

MAID. It's the one you said you stole from your wife's cupboard.

MEN. S. I never did.

MAID. Come on, don't you remember? Give me the bracelet back if you don't remember!

MEN. S. Wait! Yes, of course I remember; this is certainly the one I gave her.

MAID. That's it.

MEN. S. Where are the bangles I gave her with them?

MAID. You never gave her any bangles!

MEN. S. I did, they went together.

MAID. You did not.

MEN. S. Well, perhaps I'm wrong.

MAID. Shall I say you'll see to it?

MEN. S. Yes, tell her they'll be taken care of. She'll get the bracelet when she gets the gown.

MAID. Please, Menaechmus, give me a pair of gold earrings—about a sixteenth of an ounce—to make me glad to see you, when you visit us.

MEN. S. All right. Give me the gold, and I'll pay to have them made.

MAID. No, pay for it yourself, there's a dear, and I'll give it to you later.

MEN. S. No, give me the gold and afterwards I'll give you double.

MAID. I haven't got it.

MEN. S. Well, give it to me when you have.

MAID. Is there anything else?

MEN. S. Tell her I'll take care of these [*aside*] and sell them as soon as I can for what they'll fetch. Has she gone in? Yes, the door's shut. The gods are all ou my side, making me rich—they love me! Why wait, when I've the chance and time to escape from this lion's den? Hurry, Menaechmus, best foot forward, on your way. I'll take off my wreath and drop it here, on the left—then if they chase me they'll think I've gone that way. I'll go and find my slave, if I can, and show him what the gods have given me.

[*Exit*]

Act IV

[SPONGE *and the* WIFE *of* MENAECHMUS *of* EPIDAMNUS *appear from her house*]

WIFE. Am I to endure marriage with a man who steals everything in the house to take to his mistress?

SPONGE. Ssh! Trust me, you'll catch him red-handed. Just follow him. He went off drunk, with flowers in his hair, to take your gown he stole today to the embroiderer's. Look! That's the wreath he had on. Now am I making it up? This is the way he went, if you want to track him down. Oh! Most convenient— He's coming back. He's not carrying the gown though.

WIFE. What shall I do to him?

SPONGE. What you always do—give him hell.

WIFE. I think I will.

SPONGE. Let's get out of the way, and wait in ambush.

[MENAECHMUS *of* EPIDAMNUS *returns from the Forum*]

MEN. Our most treasured social custom is a tedious bore, and it's precisely those who are richest and most honored by their fellow citizens who hold it in most respect. They all want to collect armies of clients.[1] They never ask whether they're good men or rascals— their standing depends on something far more important than honesty. If a man's poor but respectable he's a rogue, if he's rich and a villain, he passes for an estimable client. They have no thought for the law, or what's good and right, keep their patrons on tenterhooks, take things and swear they haven't; they're avaricious, deceitful, always in court, and make their money by usury and lies. Their whole heart's in quarrelling.

[1] clients see Introduction. Not being Roman citizens they could not speak for themselves in court, but had to be represented by their patrons.

When the client appears in Court, the patron has to be there too. Just like today. A client gave me no end of trouble, and I wasn't free to choose my own actions or my own company. He hung on to me, wouldn't let me go. I had to plead for his dirty deeds before the judge, in the hope of settling the matter by asking for a payment of moneys into the Court[2] making it difficult and complicated for the other party. I said as much as I could, and what did my client do? What? Demanded a trial, and I've never seen a man more obviously guilty. There were three sharp witnesses to every crime he'd committed. Confound him! He's spoilt my lovely day. Confound me, too, for ever having set eyes on the Forum today. I got away as soon as I could. I'd ordered dinner—my lady friend's waiting for me, I know. I dare say she's angry with me, but the gown I gave her will smooth that over.

SPONGE. What have you to say?

WIFE. I've married a scoundrel.

SPONGE. Heard enough?

WIFE. Quite enough.

MEN. If I'm wise I'll go in and enjoy myself.

SPONGE. Wait! On the contrary!

MEN. Who said that? What's this? My parasite, a my wife barring the door? She's not too pleased. don't like the look of this, but I'll speak to her: W wife, what's the matter with you?

SPONGE. The fine fellow's making up to you.

MEN. Can't you stop bothering me? I wasn't talk to you, was I?

WIFE. Take your hands off me, don't touch me! S I tell you!

MEN. Why are you cross with me?

WIFE. You ought to know.

SPONGE. He does, he's only pretending, the liar.

MEN. Has one of the servants done something wr Are the maids or slaves answering back? Tell me— won't get away with it.

[2] moneys into the court he tried to postpone the trial by suading the magistrates to accept his client's bail. They willing, but the client insisted on a trial, although the ev was against him.

SPONGE. You haven't?

MEN. I certainly haven't.

SPONGE. Did you ever see such impudence? Didn't I see you standing outside that house just now, wreathed in flowers? Didn't you say my brain was addled? Didn't you say you were a stranger here, and didn't know me?

MEN. But I left you hours ago, and I've only just got back.

SPONGE. I know you. You didn't think I was capable of paying you back. I've told your wife everything.

MEN. What?

SPONGE. Ask her, I don't know.

MEN. Wife, what's this? What's he told you? What's the matter? Why don't you speak? Why don't you tell me what's up?

WIFE. As if you didn't know. Oh, I'm so miserable.

MEN. Tell me why.

WIFE. Are you asking me?

MEN. I wouldn't ask you if I knew, would I?

SPONGE. The louse, how he s making it up. You can't hide it—she knows the whole story. I told her all.

MEN. All what?

WIFE. As you're so shameless and won't own up of your own accord, stand by and listen. I'll tell you why I'm unhappy, and what he told me. My gown has been stolen from home.

MEN. My gown has been stolen?

SPONGE. See how the rogue's trying to trip you up? It was stolen from her, not you—if it had been stolen from you, it would be safe now.

MEN. I don't want anything to do with you. [To his WIFE] Now you, what are you talking about?

WIFE. I say my gown has vanished from home, you scoundrel.

MEN. Who stole it?

WIFE. He knows who stole it.

MEN. Who is it?

WIFE. Someone called Menaechmus.

MEN. That's a filthy trick. Who's this Menaechmus?

WIFE. You, I tell you.

MEN. Me?

WIFE. You.

MEN. Who says so?

WIFE. I do.

SPONGE. And I do. You gave it to your mistress Erotium.

MEN. I did?

SPONGE. Yes, you, you! Do you want an owl brought in to keep saying you, you? I'm tired of it!

MEN. Wife, I swear by Jupiter and all the gods—are you satisfied?—that I didn't give it to her.

SPONGE. And I swear I'm not lying.

MEN. But I didn't give it her for good—only lent it, as you might say.

WIFE. I don't go about lending your shirts and tunics to people. It's a woman's right to lend woman's clothes, and a man's to lend man's. Bring it back home.

MEN. All right, I will.

WIFE. I think it will be as well for you if you do. You won't set foot inside this house today, unless you bring the gown with you. I'm going home.

SPONGE. What am I going to get for letting you in on this?

WIFE. I'll do the same for you when you've been robbed.

[*Exit*]

SPONGE. That'll be never—I've nothing at home to steal. Confound husband and wife both. I'll hurry to the Forum. I can see I'll get nothing else out of this family.

[*Exit*]

MEN. My wife thinks she's done me a bad turn by locking me out—as if I didn't have the entry to a far better place! If I'm not agreeable to you, you must put up with it; I'm agreeable enough to Erotium. She won't shut me out, she'll shut me in with her. I'll go along now, and beg back the gown I gave her before—I'll give her a better one in exchange. Here, anyone at the door? Open up, and ask Erotium to step outside.

[*Enter* EROTIUM *from her house*]

EROT. Who wants me?

MEN. Somebody more his own enemy than yours.

EROT. Menaechmus! Why are you standing out here? Come in!

MEN. Just a minute. Do you know what I've come for?

EROT. Yes, for a bit of fun.

MEN. No, no. That gown I gave you earlier today— let me have it back, there's a good girl. My wife has found out everything that happened. I'll give you one twice as expensive, whichever you like.

EROT. But I gave it to you a little while ago to take to the embroiderer's, and a bracelet to go to the jeweller for remodelling.

MEN. How could you have given me the gown and a bracelet? You haven't, you know. I've only just got back since I left you and went to the Forum—I haven't seen you since.

EROT. I see what you're after. You're trying to cheat me of what I gave you.

MEN. I'm not asking for it to cheat you—I tell you my wife's found out.

EROT. I didn't ask for it, you brought it of your own accord as a present for me. Now you want it back. That's all right by me. Keep it, take it away. You and your wife can use it or lock it away. But from this day on you'll never set foot in my house again, so don't try. You owe me a lot, and you've treated me like dirt. No more credit. You can't get round me. Find yourself another woman to make a fool of.

MEN. Don't lose your temper. Here, I say, wait a minute.

[*Exit* EROTIUM]

Come back! Won't you stay still a moment? Come back, please, for my sake! She's gone in, and shut the door. I'm the most shut-out man that ever was. I'm a liar at home, and a liar to my mistress. I'll go and ask my friends what they think I ought to do.

[*Exit*]

Act V

[Enter MENAECHMUS *of* SYRACUSE *with the gown]*

MEN. S. I was a fool to give Messenio my wallet with our money in it. I dare say he's lost himself in some gambling-den.

[Enter, from her house, the WIFE*]*

WIFE. I'll see if my husband's coming back yet. There he is—I'm saved, he's got my gown.

MEN. S. I wonder where' Messenio is now.

WIFE. I'll go and give him the welcome he deserves. Aren't you ashamed to look me in the face with that gown, you good-for-nothing?

MEN. S. What's up? What's troubling you, madam?

WIFE. Have you the impudence to say one word under your breath and answer me back?

MEN. S. What have I done to be afraid to speak?

WIFE. Are you asking me? Oh, the brazen imperti nence of the man.

MEN. S. Lady, don't you know why the Greeks called Hecuba[1] a bitch?

WIFE. No.

MEN. S. Because Hecuba used to do just what you're doing now—insult everyone she met. That's how she got the name of bitch, and deserved it too.

WIFE. I can't stand your misbehavior any longer. I'd rather be single for the rest of my life than put up with the things you do.

MEN. S. What's it to me whether you're going to leave your husband or stay with him? Or is it the local custom to gossip with complete strangers?

WIFE. Gossip? I can't stand any more of this. I'd rather be an old maid than put up with your ways.

MEN. S. You can be an old maid till the day of judg ment for all I care.

---

[1] **Hecuba** wife of Priam, King of Troy. Her son Polydorus was murdered by Polymestor, King of Thrace. She revenged herself by putting out his eyes and killing his two children; afterwards she was changed into a bitch and jumped into the sea.

WIFE. I'm going to send for my father and tell him how you're treating me. [*Calls her maid*] Decio! Find my father and bring him back here with you. Tell him what's going on. [*To* MENAECHMUS] Now I'll show you up for what you are.

MEN. S. Are you insane? What have I done?

WIFE. You steal your own wife's gown and jewels for your mistress. Isn't that correct?

MEN. S. Why, you brazen hussy—you have the nerve to say I stole this from you? It was given me by another lady to have remodelled.

WIFE. You didn't deny you stole it just now. Aren't you ashamed to flaunt it before my face?

MEN. S. Now, lady, be kind—prescribe me a tonic to help me bear your bad temper, if you know one. I don't know who you think I am, but I don't know you from Eve.[2]

WIFE. Make me your laughing-stock if you like; but father's coming, you can't treat him like that. What are you staring at? Don't you know him?

MEN. S. Not from Adam.[3] I saw him the day I first saw you—today.

WIFE. You say you don't know me? You don't know father?

MEN. S. Bring your grandfather along, and I'll say the same thing to him.

WIFE. Oh, you're incorrigible.

[*Enter the* OLD MAN]

OLD MAN. I'll put my best foot forward when I have to, and try to get along as well as my age will let me. But it's not easy, make no mistake. All the hurry's gone out of me; the years have withered me up; my body's a burden, my strength's disappeared. Old age is a bad business, bad for the back, and brings all sorts of troubles when it comes. If I went through the list, I'd never stop talking. But what's on my mind to worry me at the

[2] Eve in the Latin Porthaon, grandfather of Hercules' wife, chosen here as an obscure mythological character   [3] Adam in the Latin Calchas the Greek prophet; see above

moment is why did my daughter send for me in such
a hurry? She's given me no idea what she wants or
why she's called me. But I'm pretty sure what the
trouble is—she's had a quarrel with her husband. That's
what they're like, the bitches—relying on their money[4]
to keep their husbands under their thumb. And in most
cases the men aren't blameless either. You ought only to
give a wife her own way up to a point. There was
never a girl yet sent for father but her husband had
been up to something or they'd quarrelled. Now I'll
know what the trouble is. There she is at the door, and
her husband looking upset. Just as I thought! I'll call
her over.

WIFE. I'll go and meet him. How are you, father?

OLD MAN. How are you? Do I find you in good health?
What made you send? What's upset you? Why is he
keeping his distance in a temper? I don't know what
you've been fighting about. Tell me whose fault it was,
and keep it short, I don't want a speech.

WIFE. I haven't done anything wrong, father, you
can rest easy on that score for a start. I can't stay in
this house for a minute longer. Take me home.

OLD MAN. Well, there's a fine thing!

WIFE. Father, I'm being made a laughing-stock.

OLD MAN. By whom?

WIFE. By the man you gave me to, my husband.

OLD MAN. So that's the trouble. How many times have
I told you not to bother me with your quarrels, either
of you?

WIFE. How can I help it?

OLD MAN. Do you want to know? It's easy enough if
you want to. Haven't I told you time and time again to
put up with your husband's habits, and turn a blind
eye to where he goes and what he does there?

WIFE. But he's keeping a mistress across the road.

OLD MAN. Very wise of him too. And because of all
your pains he'll love her all the more.

WIFE. But he goes drinking there.

OLD MAN. Is he going to drink less to please you

[4] **their money** their dowry, which would have to be returned
in a divorce

there or anywhere else he fancies? What do you want
to poke your nose in for? You might as well pretend to
be able to stop him dining out, or inviting his friends
home. Do you think husbands were made to wait on
you? Do you want to keep him tied to your apron
strings, or make him sit among your maids winding wool?

WIFE. I brought you here to confront him, father,
not me. You may be on my side, but you're standing up
for him.

OLD MAN. If he's done anything wrong I'll come down
much harder on him than I have on you. As long as he
does the right thing by you, and keeps you in clothes
and jewels and servants and wool to spin, it's better
to keep calm, my girl.

WIFE. But he steals my gowns and jewels from my
wardrobe—robs me, and takes my pretty things to harlots
on the sly.

OLD MAN. He's wrong if he does; if he doesn't, you're
wrong to slander an honest man.

WIFE. But father, he's got the gown now, and the
bracelet he took her—he's bringing them back because
I found out.

OLD MAN. I'll find out from him what's happened. I'll
go and speak to him. Menaechmus, let me know what
you're arguing about. What's upset you? Why is she
angry, and won't come near you?

MEN. S. Whoever you are, old man, and whatever
your name is, I call Jove on high and all the gods to
witness—

OLD MAN. Why? What on earth?

MEN. S. —that I've done her no harm. She says I stole
this from her home, swears I did. If I ever set foot in
her house, may I be the most miserable man alive.

OLD MAN. Are you mad to wish such a thing? Or to
deny you ever set foot in your own house, you lunatic?

MEN. S. Are you telling me I live there?

OLD MAN. Do you deny it?

MEN. S. I certainly do.

OLD MAN. But that's ridiculous,—unless you moved
house in your sleep. Here, my girl. Well? You haven't
moved, have you?

WIFE. Why should we? And where should we move to, pray?

OLD MAN. Don't ask me.

WIFE. He's laughing at you, don't you see? The joke's over, Menaechmus, get back to business.

MEN. S. I ask you, what have you got to do with me? Who are you? Where do you come from? Are you mad to persecute me wherever I go?

WIFE. Do you see his bloodshot eyes?[5] How green he is about the temples! How his eyes sparkle!

MEN. S. Heavens above, they're mad themselves and say I am.

WIFE. Look at him, mouthing and stretching! Oh, father, what shall I do?

OLD MAN. Come over here, my child, as far away from him as you can.

MEN. S. [Aside] The best thing I can do, if they say I'm mad, is to pretend I am, and scare them off.
Ahoy, Bacchus![6] Oh, Bromius,
Where dost thou call me to hunt in the woods?
I hear thy voice, but cannot stir from hence;
A raving bitch doth guard me on the left
And on my right a balding, aged goat
Who many a time and oft has cost
An innocent man his life through perjury.

OLD MAN. Be hanged to you!

MEN. S. Apollo's[7] oracle commands me now
With flaming torches to burn out his eyes.

OLD MAN. Oh, daughter!

WIFE. What are we to do?

OLD MAN. Suppose I call the servants here? I'll fetch people to take him away, and lock him indoors before he makes any more disturbance.

MEN. S. [Aside] Hmm, I must think—unless I can find some plan, they'll take me home with them. [Aloud] Thou biddest me plant my fists upon his face unless he go straightway out of my sight unto perdition? I'll obey, Apollo.

[5] bloodshot eyes she mistakes his anger for insanity   [6] Ahoy, Bacchus he imitates the frenzy which seized the devotees of the Wine-God; this scene parodies lines from tragedy   Bromius "the noisy one," epithet of Bacchus   [7] Apollo God of Prophecy

OLD MAN. Run home as fast as you can, before he hits you.

WIFE. I'm going. Don't let him go, father, I beg you. What an unhappy woman I am, to be spoken to like this!

[*Exit* WIFE]

MEN. S. [*Aside*] I'm rid of her without much trouble. [*Aloud*] Thou biddest me take trembling
And bearded old Methuselah,[8] dirty man,
And smash his limbs to pulp with his own staff!

OLD MAN. Touch me, and there'll be trouble. Keep your distance!

MEN. S. Thine to command, mine to obey;
I'll take an axe, and carve up his insides.

OLD MAN. I must look out—I'm beginning to be afraid of the way he's threatening me.

MEN. S. So many commands, Apollo. Thou biddest me now
Yoke two wild horses, mount my trusty car
And ride this stinking, toothless lion down.
Behold me mounted, wnip and reins in hand!
Forward, my horses, let your hoof-beats ring,
Straight on and swiftly with your racing feet!

OLD MAN. You're threatening me with a pair of horses now?

MEN. S. Once more, my Lord, you bid me ride him down
And kill him where he stands!
Ah, who plucks me by the beard? He has reversed
Thy bidding and thy commands, Apollo.

[*He collapses as if unconscious*]

OLD MAN. Oh dear, he's very ill. Heaven protect me! He was so hearty a little while ago, and now he's mad. I'll go for a doctor as fast as I can.

[*Exit*]

---

[8] **Methuselah** in the Latin Tithonus, granted immortality without eternal youth; he became first a wizened old man, then a grasshopper

MEN. S. Are they out of sight? They made a sane man mad! What am I waiting for? To the ship while it's safe. Please, everybody,[9] if the old man comes back, don't tell him which way I've gone.

[*Exit*]

[*After an interval, re-enter the* OLD MAN]

OLD MAN. My bottom's sore from sitting and my eyes from watching, waiting for the doctor to finish surgery —an objectionable man. He dragged himself away from his patients at last—says he's been mending Aesculapius' broken leg, and Apollo's arm.[10] I'm wondering whether I've hired a doctor or a stonemason. Here he comes. Hurry up that snail's pace!

[*Enter* DOCTOR]

DOC. Now, tell me, sir, what did you say his complaint was? Possession, brainstorm? Tell me, please. Any sluggishness or dropsical symptoms?

OLD MAN. That's what I'm paying you for, to tell me, and make him well again.

DOC. No trouble at all. He'll be cured, on my word of honour.

OLD MAN. I want you to be careful how you treat him.

DOC. I'll treat him so carefully he won't have another illness for years.

OLD MAN. There he is!

DOC. Let's watch how he behaves.

[*Enter* MENAECHMUS *of* EPIDAMNUS]

MEN. This has been a contrary day. Everything's gone wrong. I thought I'd get away with it, but my parasite gave the game away, and now I'm a criminal in fear of my life. My faithful henchman, ruining his lord and master! As I live and breathe, I'll murder that man to-

---

[9] **Please, everybody** he makes a direct appeal to the audience
[10] **Aesculapius, Apollo** the two Greek gods of healing. This scene parodies the conceit and jargon of the fashionable doctor.

day. No, that's stupid—it's not his life anyway, it's mine. He's been reared on my food, at my expense—I'll cut off his breath of life. That harlot has been true to type, more so, saying she'd given me the gown when I wanted it to take back to my wife again. Oh, what an unlucky man I am!

OLD MAN. Do you hear that?

Doc. He says he's unlucky.

OLD MAN. Well, go and talk to him.

Doc. How do you do, Menaechmus? Dear me, why have you uncovered your arm? Don't you know how much it aggravates the disease?

MEN. Why don't you go and hang yourself?

OLD MAN. What do you think?

Doc. What don't I think? Hellebore[11] ointment's no use in this case. Now, now, Menaechmus!

MEN. What do you want?

Doc. Answer my questions, please. Do you take your wine black?[12]

MEN. What do you want to know for? Go to the devil!

OLD MAN. That's his madness coming on.

MEN. Why don't you ask whether I eat purple bread, or yellow bread, if it comes to that? Or if I eat birds with scales or fish with feathers?

OLD MAN. Oh dear me, do you hear how he's raving? What are you waiting for? Give him some medicine, before he has a fit!

Doc. Just a moment; I have more questions to ask.

OLD MAN. This talk will be the death of him.

Doc. Tell me, are your eyes ever swollen?

MEN. What do you think I am, you clown, a lobster?

Doc. Tell me, does your stomach ever rumble, eh?

MEN. When I'm full, no; when I'm empty, yes.

Doc. He doesn't sound like a madman. Do you have a good night's rest? Do you drop off to sleep easily?

MEN. When I've no debts on my conscience. Confound you for a busybody!

[11] **Hellebore** a purgative herb used in treating insanity   [12] **Do you take your wine black** a professional question meaning "Do you take medicine in your wine?" Menaechmus takes it as nonsense.

Doc. Now he's starting to rave. Watch out when he talks like that.

OLD MAN. He's talking better than he was before— he called his wife a mad bitch!

MEN. I said what?

OLD MAN. You were mad, I tell you.

MEN. Me?

OLD MAN. Yes, you—you threatened to run me down with a four-horse chariot. I saw you; I tell you that's what you did.

MEN. And I know you stole Jupiter's sacred wreath;[13] and I know you were put in prison for it; and I know you were flogged when they let you out; and I know you killed your father and sold your mother. Satisfied? Have I slandered you as much as you've slandered me?

OLD MAN. Doctor, I implore you, whatever you're going to do, do it quickly. Can't you see he's raving mad?

Doc. Your best plan is to have him brought to me.

OLD MAN. You think so?

Doc. Why not? I'll be able to treat him there just as I please.

OLD MAN. As you like.

Doc. [*To* MENAECHMUS] Hellebore for you, for the next three weeks!

MEN. Flogging for you, for the next month! [14]

Doc. Go and get men to bring him along.

OLD MAN. How many?

Doc. No less than four, as I can see he's mad.

OLD MAN. They'll be here at once. Doctor, you watch him.

Doc. No. I'll go home, and see everything I need is ready. Tell your servants to bring him along.

OLD MAN. I'll see it's done.

Doc. I'm off now.

OLD MAN. Goodbye!

[*Exeunt*]

[13] **Jupiter's sacred wreath** his heavy sarcasm only convinces the others that he is really mad [14] **Flogging** implying that the doctor is a slave, as many were

MEN. [*To himself*] Father-in-law gone, doctor gone. I'm all alone now. Jupiter, why do they call me mad? I haven't had a day's illness since I was born. I'm not raving, I don't start fights, I don't pick quarrels; I'm sane, and can see other people are.[15] I can recognise people, and talk to them. Or are they saying I'm mad because they are? What shall I do now? I want to go home, but my wife won't let me. [*Indicating* EROTIUM's *house*] And nobody will let me in here. It's been a bad day. Well, I'll stay where I am—I'll be allowed in to-night, at any rate.

[*He sits down. Enter* MESSENIO, *obeying his master's orders to come back and meet him. He does not notice* MENAECHMUS.]

MESS. You can tell a good slave by whether he sees to his master's affairs, looks after things, keeps them in order and uses his brains; and when he protects his master's interests in his absence as well as when he's on the spot—or better; if he knows his place, he ought to think more of his back than his gullet, and more of his legs than his belly. He should remember the rewards idle, thieving, good-for-nothings get from their masters—beatings, chains, the treadmill, exhaustion, cold, starvation. That's what comes of laziness. It's my great fear. I don't mind what's said to me, but I hate being beaten, and I'd rather my corn was ground for me than have to grind it for others. So I obey my master's orders and serve him well and discreetly—I conduct myself so as to keep my back in one piece, and I'm the better for it. Let others do what they think best. I'll do what I ought to. If I stick to that, I'll keep out of trouble. As long as I'm ready whenever he wants me, I shan't have much to fear. It's nearly time for him to repay me for my services.[16] I've settled the slaves and pots in an inn, and here I am to meet him, as he ordered. I'll knock to let him know I'm here to get him safe out of this hell-hole. But I'm afraid I've come too late—the fight's over.

[15] **I'm sane . . . people are** a drunkard or madman thinks others drunk or mad and himself sober or sane [16] **repay me for my services** by setting him free

[*Enter the* OLD MAN, *with* SLAVES]

OLD MAN. In the name of heaven and humanity, listen to what I say, do as I told you, be careful, use your heads. Pick him up and carry him to the doctor, if you value your limbs and hides. Watch out for his threats, he won't care a straw for the lot of you. What's keeping you? Why don't you move? You ought to have him off his feet by this time. I'll go to the doctor, and be waiting for him when you arrive.

[*The* SLAVES *advance on the unsuspecting* MENAECHMUS, *who suddenly sees them coming*]

MEN. Murder! What's going on? Why are they after me? What do you want? What are you looking for? What are you doing behind my back?

[*They pick him up and carry him away*]

Where are you taking me? Where are you going? I'm being killed! People of Epidamnus, protect me! Help! Help! A rape! A rape!

MESS. Almighty gods, what do I see here? Strangers carrying off my master as if he were nobody!

MEN. Hasn't anyone got pluck enough to help me?

MESS. All the pluck in the world, master!

[*He leaps to his defence*]

Oh people of Epidamnus, the scandal, the disgrace! To think that a man who came here a free citizen should be manhandled in the street, in a peaceful town, in broad daylight!

MEN. Whoever you are, give me a hand—don't let them get away with this.

MESS. I'll give you a hand, I'll help you, I'll come to your aid with all my heart. I'd die myself before I let any harm come to you. Gouge out the eyes of that one who's got you on his shoulder, master—I'll give the rest a thrashing, I'll plant my fists on their faces. You'll pay for kidnapping this man today.

MEN. I've got his eye.

MESS. Then have it out! Robbers, thieves, pirates!

SLAVES. Murder! Let us go!

MESS. Drop him, then.

MEN. Take your hands off me. Come on, put your fists up!

MESS. Go on, get out. Run away and be hanged.

[*All the* SLAVES *run away except one*]

Oh, are you still there? There's a prize for being last!

[*Beats him. Exit* SLAVE.]

Just as I'd hoped. I've got the measure of their faces pretty well. So, master, I came to help you in the nick of time!

MEN. Heaven bless you the rest of your days, young fellow, whoever you are. If it hadn't been for you I wouldn't have lived to see the sun go down.

MESS. Well, do what's right, and give me my freedom.

MEN. Your freedom?

MESS. Yes, since I've given you yours.

MEN. What? You're making a mistake, young man.

MESS. What mistake?

MEN. I swear by Father Jupiter I'm not your master.

MESS. Don't say that!

MEN. I'm not lying—no slave of mine has ever done for me what you've just done.

MESS. Then if I'm not your property, as you say, let me go free.

MEN. You're free as far as I'm concerned—go where you like.

MESS. You really mean it?

MEN. Of course—as far as it's up to me to tell you anything.

MESS. Hail, patron! [17] You free me in all seriousness, I accept in all happiness.

MEN. I believe you.

MESS. But, patron, I beg you, order me about just like when I was your slave. I'll live with you, and go home with you. Wait for me—I'll go to the inn, and get the pots and the money. The wallet with our fare is sealed up in my bag. I'll be straight back with it.

[17] **Hail patron** once freed he becomes Menaechmus' client

MEN. See that you are.

MESS. I'll give it back just as you gave it me, untouched. Wait here.

[Exit]

MEN. Some very strange things have happened to me today. For one, this fellow I've just set free claims he's my slave. He says he'll bring me a purse of money. If he does, I'll tell him he's free to go where he likes, in case he wants it back when he comes to his senses. My father-in-law and the doctor say I'm mad. It's very strange, whatever it is. It seems more like a dream than anything else. Now I'll pay that slut a visit, though she is angry with me, to see if I can't persuade her to give me the gown to take home.

[*Exit into* EROTIUM's *house. Enter* MENAECHMUS *of* SYRA-CUSE *and* MESSENIO, *quarrelling.*]

MEN. S. What a nerve! You dare to say you've already met me today, after I told you to come and meet me here?

MESS. Yes, and what's more I rescued you from four men who were kidnapping you in front of this house. You were calling on heaven and earth when I came along and fought to get you away against their will. And because of that, because I saved you, you set me free. When I said I'd go for the money and the luggage, you ran as fast as you could to cut me off, just to go back on what you said.

MEN. S. I said you could go free?

MESS. You did.

MEN. S. You can be sure of one thing—I'll be a slave myself before I let you loose.

[*Enter* MENAECHMUS *of* EPIDAMNUS, *shouting at* ERO-TIUM *and the* MAID *inside the house*]

MEN. E. Swear by your eyes as much as you like, you won't make it any more true that I took the gown and bracelet, you hussies.

MESS. Almighty gods, what's this I see?

MEN. S. What?

MESS. Your reflection!

MEN. S. What's going on?

MESS. Your living image!

MEN. S. Well, he's not unlike, when you look at me.

MEN. E. [*To* MESSENIO] Bless you for protecting me, young fellow, whoever you are.

MESS. Tell me your name, sir, if you please—unless you don't like to.

MEN. E. It would be less than you deserved, if I were ashamed of telling you what you wanted. My name's Menaechmus.

MEN. S. No, it's mine.

MEN. E. I'm a Sicilian, from Syracuse.

MEN. S. The same town and country as me.

MEN. E. What's this I hear?

MEN. S. The truth.

MESS. [*Indicating* MENAECHMUS *of* EPIDAMNUS] I know this man! He's my master, I'm his slave—[*Indicating* MENAECHMUS *of* SYRACUSE]—and I thought I was his! I thought he was you, and gave him all that trouble. [*To* MENAECHMUS *of* SYRACUSE] Please forgive me if I forgot my place and said anything I shouldn't.

MEN. S. You're raving. Don't you remember coming ashore with me this morning?

MESS. That's a fair question. You're my master—you must find another slave. Sir, at your service—sir, leaving yours. This is Menaechmus.

MEN. E. But I'm Menaechmus!

MEN. S. What are you talking about? You're Menaechmus?

MEN. E. I am, I tell you. My father was Moschus.

MEN. S. You're my father's son?

MEN. E. No. I'm my own father's son. I don't want yours.

MESS. Immortal gods, who could have hoped for this! Grant my suspicions are correct! Either I'm going mad, or these two are the twin brothers. They claim the same country and the same father. I'll call my master aside. Menaechmus!

BOTH. What do you want?

MESS. Not both of you—my master. Which of you came here by ship with me?

MEN. E. Not me.

MEN. S. I did.

MESS. Then it's you I want, come here.

MEN. S. Here I am. Well?

MESS. Either that man's a fraud or he's your twin brother. I've never seen two men more alike. Believe me, you're as like as water to water or milk to milk. And on top of that he claims the same father and birthplace. The best thing is for us to go and question him.

MEN. S. You've given me good advice and I'm grateful. Go ahead, see to it, there's a good fellow. If you find he is my brother, you're a free man.

MESS. I hope so!

MEN. S. So do I.

MESS. [*To* MENAECHMUS *of* EPIDAMNUS] Well, now, I think you said your name was Menaechmus.

MEN. E. So it is.

MESS. His name is Menaechmus too. You said you were born in Sicily, in Syracuse. He was born there too. You said your father was Moschus. So was his. Now you can both listen to me, and to each other.

MEN. E. You've deserved so well of me I'll do whatever you ask. Free though I am, I'm your willing slave, as much as if you'd bought me.

MESS. I'm hoping to discover that you're twin brothers, born of one mother and one father, on the same day.

MEN. E. That's incredible! If you could only do what you've promised!

MESS. I can. Now, each of you answer my questions.

MEN. E. Ask when you like—I'll answer, and won't keep back anything I know.

MESS. Is your name Menaechmus?

MEN. E. It is.

MESS. And is yours the same?

MEN. S. Yes.

MESS. You say Moschus was your father?

MEN. E. He was.

MEN. S. And mine.

MESS. Are you a Syracusan?

MEN. E. Of course.

MESS. And you?

MEN. S. Why not?

MESS. All the indications agree so far. Now pay attention again. What's your earliest memory of your country?

MEN. E. When my father took me to Tarentum[18] on a trading voyage, I wandered away from him in the crowd, and was brought here.

MEN. S. Jove in the highest, protect me!

MESS. What are you shouting at? Be quiet! [*To* ME-NAECHMUS *of* EPIDAMNUS] How old were you, when your father took you from home?

MEN. E. Seven. I was just losing my first teeth. That was the last time I saw my father.

MESS. Now, how many sons did your father have?

MEN. E. Two, to the best of my recollection.

MESS. Which was the elder, you or your brother?

MEN. E. We were the same age.

MESS. How's that?

MEN. E. We were twins.

MEN. S. The gods are with me!

MESS. If you interrupt, I won't say another word.

MEN. S. No, no, I'll be quiet.

MESS. Tell me, did you both have the same name?

MEN. E. Far from it. I was Menaechmus, as I am now, and they called him Sosicles.

MEN. S. It's all clear—I can't contain myself, let me embrace you! My twin brother! I'm Sosicles!

MEN. E. Then how did you come by the name Menaechmus?

MEN. S. When you and my father were reported dead, grandfather changed my name and gave me yours.

MEN. E. I believe it's as you say! But tell me—

MEN. S. Ask away.

MEN. E. What was mother's name?

MEN. S. Teuximarcha.

MEN. E. It's all right! Oh, welcome, my long-lost brother, I'd never hoped to find you.

MEN. S. And I'm overjoyed to find you—I've been to great trouble and hardship to look for you.

MESS. This is why that harlot called you by his name.

[18] **Tarentum** important Greek colony in Southern Italy

She thought you were him, I suppose, when she invited you to dinner.

MEN. E. Here! I ordered dinner for myself today, without my wife knowing. I stole her gown from home this morning, and gave it to her.

MEN. S. You mean the one I've got here?

MEN. E. How did you get it?

MEN. S. The harlot who took me to dinner said I gave it to her. I had a good meal, drank well, and went to bed with her. She then gave me this gown and some gold.

MEN. E. I'm glad I brought you luck. When she asked you in, I suppose she took you for me.

MESS. Need I wait any longer for my freedom, as you promised?

MEN. E. He couldn't make a better or fairer request, brother; let him go, for my sake.

MEN. S. You're free!

MEN. E. I'm glad you're free, Messenio.

MESS. [*Aside*] But I'll need better security than that, before I'm free for good.[19]

MEN. S. Since everything's turned out as we hoped, brother, let's go back home together.

MEN. E. Brother, I'll do as you wish. I'll hold an auction here and sell all I have. And in the meantime, brother, let's go inside.

MEN. S. By all means.

MESS. Do you know what I'd like to ask you?

MEN. E. What?

MESS. Let me be auctioneer.[20]

MEN. E. With all my heart.

MESS. Do you want it announced at once?

MEN. E. For today week.

[*The* BROTHERS *go in.* MESSENIO *advances to the front of the stage and addresses the audience.*]

MESS. The auction of Menaechmus' goods will be held on the morning of today week! Sale of slaves, furniture,

---

[19] **better security** he needs money as well, to set himself up
[20] **auctioneer** a profitable profession, and popular among freedmen

estate, and property! All to go to the highest bidder, ready money only! Sale of wife, too, if anyone wants to buy her! I doubt if the whole lot will fetch five million sesterces! [21]

Now goodnight, audience—and applaud us well.[22]

[21] **five million sesterces** an absurdly large sum   [22] **applaud us well** the invariable ending to Roman comedy, spoken either by the actor who speaks last or by some other member of the troupe

BIBLIOGRAPHY

❧

THE ANCIENT THEATER

Beare, W., *The Roman Stage* (Methuen, London, 1950).

Bieber, M., *The History of the Greek and Roman Theater* (Princeton, 1939).

Flickinger, R. C., *The Greek Theater and its Drama* (Chicago, 1936).

Harsh, P. W., *A Handbook of Classical Drama* (Stanford, 1944). Plot-summaries and biographical information.

TEXTS AND TRANSLATIONS

Aristophanes, *Comedies*, ed. F. W. Hall and W. M. Geldart, 2 vols. (Oxford, 1906). Greek text with critical apparatus.

Aristophanes, *Comedies*, ed. B. B. Rogers, 11 vols. (London, 1907-30). Greek text, commentary, and verse translation. The *Plutus* also contains a translation of the *Menaechmi*.

Plautus, *Comedies*, ed. W. M. Lindsay, 2 vols. (Oxford, 1908). Latin text with critical apparatus.

Plautus, *Comedies*, trans. P. Nixon, Loeb Classical Library, 5 vols. (New York and Harvard (Vol. 5), 1916-1951). Latin text with facing English translation.

The Complete Roman Drama, ed. G. E. Duckworth, 2 vols. (Random House, New York, 1942). Translations from various sources.

Plautus, *Menaechmi*, ed. N. Mosely and M. Hammond (Harvard, 1946). Latin text with notes.

ANALYSIS AND CRITICISM

Cornford, F. M., *The Origin of Attic Comedy* (Edward Arnold, London, 1914).

105

Duckworth, G. E., *The Nature of Roman Comedy: a study in popular entertainment* (Princeton, 1952).

Lever, K., *The Art of Greek Comedy* (Methuen, London, 1956).

Murray, G., *Aristophanes* (Oxford, 1933).

Norwood, G., *Greek Comedy* (Methuen, London, 1931).